W9-CBN-569

Unemployment and Macroeconomics

The Ohlin Lectures

Unemployment and Macroeconomics

Assar Lindbeck

The MIT Press
Cambridge, Massachusetts
London, England

This book was set in Palatino by Asco Trade Typesetting Ltd., Hong Kong and was printed and bound in the United States of America.

Library of Congress Cataloging-in-Publication Data

Lindbeck, Assar.
    Unemployment and macroeconomics / Assar Lindbeck.
        p.   cm.—(The Ohlin lectures; 3)
    "Ohlin lectures, Handelshögskolan i Stockholm (Stockholm School of Economics), November 1989."
    Includes bibliographical references and index.
    ISBN 0-262-12175-1
    1. Unemployment. 2. Employment (Economic theory)
3. Macroeconomics. 4. Microeconomics. 5. Economic policy. 6. Full employment policies. 7. Business cycles. I. Title. II. Series.
HD5707.5.L564 1993
559.5—dc20   92-29465
                                                                      CIP

Contents

Tables and Figures

Tables

Figures

Acknowledgments

This book is a revised version of the Ohlin Lectures, which I was privileged to give at the Stockholm School of Economics (Handelshögskolan i Stockholm) in November 1989.

Many ideas in the book have grown out of earlier collaboration with Dennis Snower. I am grateful for comments on an earlier draft of the manuscript by Thorvaldur Gylfason, Harald Lang, Petter Lundvik, Larry Summers, and three anonymous referees. I thank Magnus Dahlquist and Joakim Persson for assistance with the empirical data. Lotta Änggård patiently typed various versions of the manuscript. Julie Sundqvist checked the language. John Hassler and Torbjörn Becker have assisted with proofreading and also provided helpful comments. A great deal of the work on this book was done while I was visiting the Research Department of the International Monetary Fund, Washington, D.C., in 1990.

Unemployment and Macroeconomics

1   Introduction

This small book deals with employment and unemployment in a macroeconomic framework. The purpose is not, however, to give a comprehensive survey of the field. The aim is, rather, to argue in favor of a specific approach, with a nonequilibrating labor market in the center of the analysis. Discussions of other approaches are pursued for reasons of comparison.

As a consequence of the macroeconomic approach of the book, I do not analyze the fine structure of employment and unemployment. Accordingly, very little is said about job search, vacancies and mismatch between demand and supply of labor, the incidence of unemployment on different groups of employees, and so forth. (For a more comprehensive analysis of such phenomena, see, for instance, Layard, Nickell, and Jackman 1991b.) Instead, the book investigates the microfoundations of unemployment and discusses the microeconomic incentives and opportunities for unemployed workers. This encompasses such issues as the hiring and firing of labor, the market power of incumbent workers, the design of unemployment benefit systems, the organization of wage bargaining, labor market training and exchange systems, and public sector employment programs.

Against the background of the unemployment experience of developed market economies during the last century, and in particular after World War II (surveyed in chapter 2), the book is organized around three main questions:

1. Why does unemployment exist at all, and how are aggregate employment and unemployment determined (chapters 3 and 4)?

2. What are the initial impulses ("shocks") that from time to time precipitate changes in the levels of aggregate employment and unemployment, and how are these shocks transmitted to the labor market (chapters 5 and 6)?

3. How do we explain the apparent persistence of unemployment, often even after reversal of the initial impulse that precipitated the change in unemployment (chapter 7)?

The last chapter summarizes the answers to these questions and considers the main policy implications of the analysis.

Because unemployment cannot be analyzed in a serious manner without raising some basic methodological issues, this study deals with problems of substance and methodology simultaneously, although with the hope of avoiding becoming bogged down by technicalities. One basic methodological issue is how the labor market, including wage formation, should be modeled realistically and integrated into macroeconomic theory. A closely related methodological issue is how product demand and supply shocks are transmitted to the labor market. The three basic questions I have posed cannot be answered without dealing with these methodological issues.

There has been a tendency among scholars in macroeconomics to start "from scratch," over and over again, largely neglecting, and indeed often explicitly denying, previous analytical achievements. In the first decades after World War II, Keynesians tended to throw out previous macroeconomic contributions by classical economists, from David Hume to Friedrich von Hayek, and in the 1970s the new classical macroeconomists tended to deny the achievements of Keynesian-oriented macroeconomists.

One reason for this outlook toward the achievements of preceding generations of macroeconomists may be that it is easier to highlight a new idea if it is elaborated in an extreme form and if no attempt is made to integrate it with previously accumulated insights. Lately, however, there have been serious attempts to bring about such an integration. Thus, another ambition of this book is to embed attempted original contributions into analytical structures and accumulated insights that have been developed by others, even if it is not possible to do full justice to other approaches in a short book.

Although the book is mainly theoretical, I apply the analysis to real-world situations in various Organization of Economic Cooperation and Development (OECD) countries. These applications refer not only to large countries, or groups of countries, like the United States, the United Kingdom and the European Community (EC) as a whole, but also to the Scandinavian countries, which provide interesting experiences of the unemployment issue and of policies to fight unemployment. Sweden's full employment policy, which has attracted much international interest, is given particular attention, largely because this experience has, in my view, been grossly misunderstood, especially by foreign observers.

2   The Empirical Picture

As a background to the analysis in this book of the causes and mechanisms of unemployment, it is useful to establish some facts regarding the unemployment experience in various developed countries.

Let us start with a very long-term perspective, covering an entire century. (The deficiencies in the quality of the data imply that they can provide only a rough description of the unemployment experience.) I concentrate on six aspects: (1) the distinction between (more or less) regular business cycles and unique historical events; (2) the presence or absence of long-term trends in the aggregate unemployment rate; (3) the persistence of aggregate unemployment and the duration of unemployment spells of individual workers; (4) differences in country experiences of unemployment; (5) the relation between unemployment and inflation; and (6) the covariation of aggregate employment and the unemployment rate.

Business Cycles Versus Unique Historical Events

Time series of unemployment rates, illustrated in figure 2.1 for eight developed countries, look like stochastic processes with

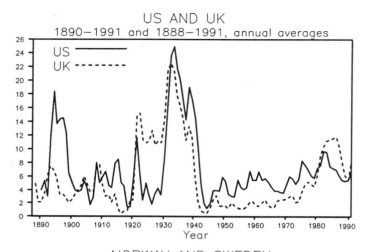

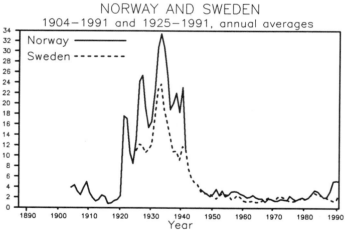

Figure 2.1
Unemployment rate. Sources: U.S. Department of Commerce, Bureau of the Census, *USA Historical Statistics, Colonial Times*, tables D-85-86 (from 1890 to 1970), and OECD, *Economic Outlook*, no. 44, 48, 49 (from 1971 to 1991).

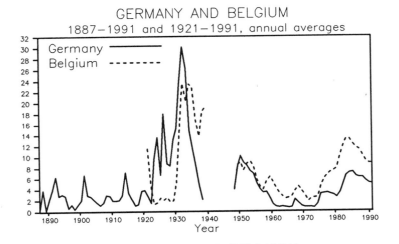

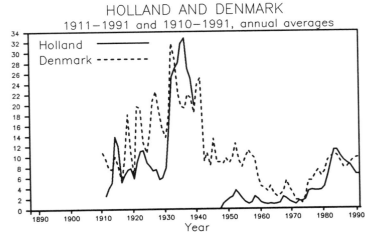

Figures for 1991 are OECD projections. European countries: B. R. Michell, *European Historical Statistics 1750–1975*, 2d rev. ed. (New York: Macmillan, 1980). Figures for 1991 are OECD projections.

high probabilities of small disturbances and low probabilities of huge disturbances. While the former may reasonably be interpreted as reflecting traditional business cycles, the latter seem to be related to easily identifiable unique historical events, often connected with dramatic policy actions by governments. Obvious examples of such events are the deflationary monetary and exchange rate policies in the early 1920s in some countries (such as the United Kingdom), when central banks reverted to the gold standard at the old exchange rate parity; the worldwide depression in the early 1930s, which was, if not initiated then at least accentuated by restrictive monetary policies and trade restrictions; and the oil price hikes that were initiated by the OPEC (Organization of Petroleum Exporting Countries) governments in 1973 and 1979, as well as the subsequent anti-inflationary economic policies of the governments in several large OECD countries, in particular after the 1979 oil price shock.

Figure 2.1 also illustrates the pronounced differences in the average level of unemployment during various multiyear periods, such as during the course of different business cycles. Indeed, these differences are much larger than the variations in the unemployment rate within each cycle.[1] It therefore seems to be more important to explain prolonged periods of high unemployment (possibly lasting for an entire decade), often in connection with, or after, unique historical events, than the relatively modest short-term fluctuations in the unemployment rate associated with ordinary business cycles.

Absence of Long-Term Trends in Unemployment Rate

Another striking feature of time series of unemployment rates, which is also suggested by figure 2.1, is the apparent absence of a trend in the very long run (over several decades or even a century), at least until the 1980s. The number of employed workers seems to have developed in parallel with the labor force over the very long run, in spite of the pronounced long-run upward trend of both labor productivity and the labor force. In this sense, we might refer to the rule of Say's Law in the very long run. This experience suggests that a realistic macroeconomic theory of unemployment has to be consistent with an unemployment rate that is independent, in the long run, of both labor productivity and the size of the labor force. However, basic changes in the structure of the economy—for instance, changes in the composition of the labor force, in search technology, in the functioning of the housing market, in the generosity of the unemployment benefit system, and in the aggressiveness of unions—would certainly be expected to influence the unemployment level.

Unemployment Persistence

In spite of the apparent tendency for the unemployment rate to return to some long-run "normal" level, time series of unemployment rates do suggest unemployment persistence, in the sense that the unemployment rate in year t is positively correlated with the unemployment rate in year $t - 1$ (and usually also with the rate in one or a few previous years),

$$u_t = au_{t-1} + \varepsilon_t, \tag{2.1}$$

in the simplest case with one time lag. The unemployment rate in period t is u_t, and ε_t is a random disturbance term ("white noise") with the expected value zero and constant variance. The coefficient $a \geqslant 0$ expresses the strength of the persistence effect. According to the celebrated "hysteresis hypothesis," coefficient a would be unity (the unit root hypothesis), implying that the macroeconomy systematically (that is, except for random disturbances) would tend to be "stuck" at whatever unemployment rate happens to exist. (The unemployment rate in this extreme case would be a random walk; that is, the expected value of the unemployment rate in one period would be the actual rate in the period immediately preceding it.) In fact, if such a hysteresis theory were correct, the unemployment rate would equally likely tend to rise toward 100 percent as to decline toward zero, which is rather implausible. In view of the tendency for the unemployment rate to return to some normal interval, the empirical evidence (as illustrated in figure 2.1) does not suggest that persistence is that strong. Most formal time-series studies of unemployment rates by various authors also seem to contradict the (strong) hysteresis hypothesis (Coe and Gagliardi 1985; Wyplosz 1987; Layard, Nickell, and Jackman 1991b, pp. 412–413).[2]

It is often argued that the unemployment rate has a stronger tendency to be stuck at extreme peaks than at more modest ("local") peaks; in other words, the unemployment persistence is particularly pronounced when unemployment is exceptionally high. However, on rough inspection, the statistics depicted in figure 2.1 hardly give a strong impression of such a relation. Indeed, according to these data, the speed (in both percentage points and in percentage) at which the unemployment rate moves toward more "normal" long-term rates turns out, in general, to be at least as fast when starting from extreme peaks as from normal recession peaks. Of course, it takes longer for the unemployment rate to return to the long-term normal rate in the former case because the unemployment rate then has a longer distance to travel. However, this observation provides no grounds for asserting that unemployment persistence is stronger at exceptionally high unemployment rates than at more normal rates.

As an illustration, figure 2.1 suggests that unemployment fell quite fast from the high peaks in the 1930s, although unemployment was very high during most of that decade due to a double peak of the unemployment rate in some countries. It is perhaps tempting to interpret the experiences in the EC area in the 1980s as a tendency toward particularly stubborn persistence at high levels of unemployment. However, we could equally well argue that unemployment persistence has been particularly high during periods of low unemployment, such as in the period 1950–1970.

It is well known that strong increases in unemployment, at least in Western Europe, have usually been connected with a fall in the outflow rate from the unemployment pool rather than with a sharp increase in the inflow to the unemployment pool. The duration of average unemployment spells also tends to rise with higher aggregate unemployment, after an initial fall in average duration in the early phase of a period of higher aggregate unemployment. Moreover, because the same individual often becomes unemployed more than once during a given year, unemployment has usually been confined to a rather small fraction of the population in both Western Europe and the United States.

Another well-known observation is that manual and unskilled workers have a higher propensity to be unemployed than white-collar workers. It is also well established that the youngest, and sometimes also the oldest, workers tend to experience more unemployment than middle-aged men (in the same types of professions).

Country Differences

Good theories of unemployment should be consistent with, and explain, facts such as those I have noted. Ideally, they should also help explain the pronounced differences in the unemployment experience among countries. Although changes in unemployment rates over time are rather closely correlated among countries—probably because of the international character of macroeconomic shocks, intercountry transmission of domestic shocks, or similar trends in economic policies actually pursued —it is a commonplace that the unemployment experience varies drastically among countries.

Two marked differences between employment performance in the United States and the EC countries were observed during the first twenty-five years after World War II: (1) the general level of measured unemployment was considerably higher in the United States, usually 4 to 6 percent as compared to 2 to 3 percent in most EC countries,[3] and (2) short-term (cyclical) fluctuations in employment and unemployment were larger in the United States than in Western Europe (figure 2.2). The observation of larger cyclical fluctuations in unemployment in the United States also holds when the fluctuations are measured relative to fluctuations in aggregate output.[4] Although the aggregate employment performance of Japan in this period was closer to the Western European than to the U.S. pattern, a specific feature of the Japanese experience was extremely small fluctuations in (un)employment relative to fluctuations in aggregate output.[5]

In view of these empirical observations, in the 1950s and 1960s it was often argued that macroeconomic stability was superior,

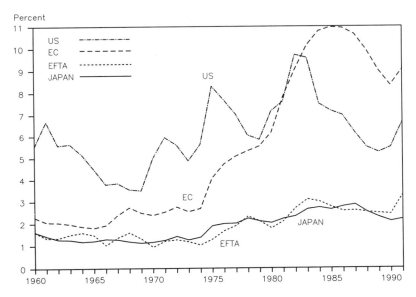

Figure 2.2
Unemployment, 1960–1991 (in groups of countries). Source: OECD, *Economic Outlook*, no. 49 (July 1991). Note: Country weights (for EC and EFTA) from labor force statistics.

and the labor market functioned "better," in Western Europe and Japan than in the United States. While the employment experience in Japan continued to be impressive after the mid-1970s, the conventional assessment of the relative performance of the United States and Western Europe was largely reversed in the 1980s. The reasons were the much stronger cyclical recovery of aggregate employment from the deep recessions of the mid-1970s and early 1980s in the United States than in Western Europe and the related lower average unemployment rate in the United States than in Western Europe in the 1980s.

These experiences are obvious illustrations of less unemployment persistence in the United States than in Western Europe. Indeed, formal statistical measures of unemployment persistence in terms of autoregressive time-series analysis by various authors are consistent with this observation (Blanchard and Summers 1986; Alogoskoufis and Manning 1988).

The relative deterioration of employment performance in Western Europe, as compared to the United States and Japan in the 1970s and 1980s, was even more pronounced than indicated by these observations. First, there seems to have been a much larger increase in what is sometimes called hidden unemployment in Western Europe than in the United States during this period. One indication is the fall in labor force participation rates in many European countries, not only by way of early retirement but also through the emergence of so-called discouraged workers—those who have basically stopped searching for jobs. While both the labor force and aggregate employment grew by about 2 percent per year in the United States during the 1970s and 1980s, aggregate employment in Western Europe grew, on the average, by only about 0.5 percent per year while the labor force grew by 0.8 percent per year.[6] Second, in Western Europe there was a considerable increase in invisible unemployment in the sense that, to a larger extent than before, people were forced to work fewer hours than they would have liked at going wage rates, for instance, in the form of compulsory work sharing (OECD *Employment Outlook*, September 1987).

After six years of annual output growth of 1.9 percent in Western Europe during the period 1979–1985, there was barely any overall increase in aggregate employment. Much more rapid employment growth in the United States than in Western

Europe was achieved with only marginally faster output growth (table 2.1). It was only after five additional years of fairly brisk economic growth (3.0 percent per year) in Western Europe as a whole in the period 1985–1990 that there was a significant increase in aggregate employment (by 1.3 percent per year) and a fall in unemployment.

These figures reflect the fact that labor productivity growth was much weaker in the United States than in the EC countries during the 1970s and 1980s (table 2.1, column 3). An interpretation along standard economic theory lines would be that the U.S. labor market reacted to the rapid growth of the labor force during this period by way of stagnation in real wages (table 2.1, columns 4 and 5) and that this stimulated labor-intensive output growth, which explains the sluggish growth of labor productivity. In this sense, the U.S. labor market may have reacted in a very "rational" way to the rapid increase in the labor force. The drastic rise in aggregate employment, stagnation of real wages, and slow labor productivity growth would be elements of one and the same process. (I return to this issue in chapter 8 in the context of country experiences of real wage flexibility.)

The contrasts between the United States and Western Europe as a whole should not obscure the sharp differences among various European countries. In particular, it is a challenge to explain the relatively low unemployment rates during most of the 1970s and 1980s in a group of small countries that all happen to belong to EFTA (European Free Trade Area): Austria, Norway, Sweden, Switzerland, and (to a lesser extent) Finland (figure 2.2 and table 2.2). Did the favorable unemployment experiences in this group of countries in the 1970s and 1980s depend on specific long-term institutional features of these countries, or were they the result of specific short-term policies?

Table 2.1
Growth rates of GNP, employment, labor productivity, real consumption wage, and real product wage (annual rate of growth, in percentage)

	(1) GNP	(2) Employ- ment	(3) Labor productivity (per capita)	(4) Consump- tion real wages	(5) Real product wage (per employed)
United States					
1973−1979	3.0	2.7	0.0	0.1	0.0
1979−1985	2.2	1.6	0.7	−1.0	0.6
1985−1990	2.9	2.0	1.2	−0.9[a]	0.8[a]
1973−1990	2.7	2.0	0.6	−0.4[a]	0.4[a]
Western Europe					
1973−1979	3.0	0.4	2.4	3.0	4.6
1979−1985	1.9	0.1	1.6	0.4	1.2
1985−1990	3.0	1.3	1.7	1.7[a]	3.8[a]
1973−1990	2.5	0.6	1.9	1.8[a]	3.2[a]

a. Up to 1989.
Notes: The definition of Western Europe in columns 1−3 corresponds to OECD Europe. Countries included in the Western European figures for columns 4−5 are: Austria, Belgium, Denmark, Finland, France, Germany, Italy, the Netherlands, Norway, Switzerland, Sweden, and United Kingdom. Switzerland, however, is excluded from column 5.
Sources: Columns 1−2 are based on OECD *Economic Outlook*, no. 49. Column 3 is based on OECD, *Historical Statistics, 1960−1989*, and for 1990 on OECD, *Economic Outlook*, no. 49. Columns 4 and 5 are based on the Swedish Employers' Confederation's International Survey, "Wages and Total Labor Costs for Workers," and on OECD, *Historical Statistics, 1960−1989*.

Table 2.2
Unemployment in OECD countries, 1960–1991 (percentage)

	1960–68	1969–73	1974–79	1980–85	1986–90	Third quarter 1991
European Community						
Belgium	2.3	2.4	6.3	11.3	9.5	7.8
Denmark	2.0	1.4	5.5	9.3	8.6	10.7
France	1.7	2.6	4.5	8.3	9.8	9.5
West Germany	0.7	0.8	3.2	6.0	5.9	4.6
Ireland	5.0	5.6	7.6	12.6	16.2	15.8
Italy	3.8	4.2	4.6	6.4	7.7	9.6
Netherlands	1.2	2.0	5.1	10.1	8.8	6.6
Spain	2.4	2.7	5.3	16.6	18.7	16.3
United Kingdom	2.6	3.4	5.1	10.5	8.8	9.9
Oceania						
Australia	2.2	2.0	5.0	7.6	7.2	9.9
New Zealand	0.2	0.3	0.8	3.9	5.6	10.7
North America						
Canada	4.7	5.6	7.2	9.9	8.3	10.4
United States	4.7	4.9	6.7	8.0	5.8	6.7
Japan	1.4	1.2	1.9	2.4	2.5	2.2
EFTA						
Austria	1.6	1.1	1.5	3.0	3.4	4.7
Finland	1.8	2.3	4.4	5.1	4.3	8.2
Norway	2.0	1.7	1.8	2.6	3.5	5.5
Sweden	1.3	1.8	1.5	2.4	1.7	2.8
Switzerland	0.1	0.0	1.0	1.7	1.9	1.4

Notes: All figures are standardized measures of unemployment, except for Denmark, Austria, and Switzerland.
Sources: OECD, *Main Economic Indicators* (January 1992).

In the latter case, it would also be important to ascertain whether these policies can be sustained. This issue is highlighted by a rather dramatic increase in unemployment rates in some of these countries during the late 1980s and early 1990s: in Norway from 1.5 to 5 percent during the two-year period 1986–1987, in Finland from 3.5 to 13 percent between early 1990 and mid-1992, and in Sweden from 1.5 to 5 percent from mid-1990 to mid-1992.

There are also a number of country differences in the nature of unemployment. One example is the length of unemployment spells. More specifically, whereas the average length of (unterminated) unemployment spells in North America, Japan, Austria, Norway, and Sweden was two to six months in the mid-1980s, they were often as high as a year, or even more, in some EC countries (column 2 in table 2.3).[7] Indeed, such differences also seem to exist in situations where the level and previous time path of aggregate unemployment are about the same in various countries (OECD *Employment Outlook*, 1987).

These differences in unemployment experiences in the 1980s have profoundly influenced economists' views on how the macroeconomy and the labor market operate in various countries. Perhaps more important, the general conception of what is regarded as desirable and undesirable features of labor markets has changed. Generally, large cyclical fluctuations in employment and unemployment (low unemployment persistence) were regarded as a sign of deplorable macroeconomic and labor market instability during the first twenty-five years after World War II. By the 1980s, when the U.S. economy bounced back from recessions rather fast while Western Europe experienced persistently high unemployment, the performance of the U.S. labor market tended to be regarded as an example of flexibility.

Table 2.3
Unemployment rates and duration, 1986

	Unemployment rate (%)	Duration (months)
European Community		
France	10.4	19.2
Germany	6.4	8.2
Ireland	17.4	11.2
Netherlands	9.9	23.3
Spain	21.0	34.5
United Kingdom	11.3	8.6
North America		
Canada	9.5	3.6
United States	6.9	2.4
Japan	2.8	5.4
EFTA		
Austria	3.1	5.0
Norway	2.0	2.7
Sweden	2.7	3.8

Note: Unemployment duration is defined here as the average length of unterminated spells.
Source: WIDER World Economy Group 1989 Report.

As a consequence, while politicians and labor market specialists went to Western Europe during the earlier period to learn about the wonders of the labor markets in that part of the world, by the 1980s European labor market specialists and politicians began to envy the "flexibility" of the U.S. labor market. If unemployment in the EC countries returns to historically more normal levels in the 1990s after the relatively high levels of the 1980s, various observers may again tend to regard large fluctuations in employment and unemployment (that is, low persistence) as having negative connotations.

It is an important analytical task to explore these differences in unemployment experiences among countries. In particular, to what extent do they depend on differences in macroeconomic policies and institutional arrangements, respectively?

Relation between Unemployment and Inflation

My interpretation of time series of unemployment and inflation (including a comparision of figures 2.2 and 2.3), and of econometric studies of such time series, is that the basic idea behind the traditional Phillips curve hypothesis is correct in the sense that there is a short-term partial (ceteris paribus) relation between unemployment and inflation, at least at relatively low levels of unemployment and provided fluctuations in unemployment are driven by demand shocks. It is also, I believe, reasonable to interpret this Phillips curve relation in the manner of Phillips and Lipsey: as nominal wage increases being driven by the excess demand (supply) situation in the labor market rather than according to Robert Lucas's alternative interpretation, in which unexpected and misinterpreted wage and price changes generate fluctuations in output and employment.

As ceteris is seldom paribus, it is hardly surprising that even the inflation-augmented (or expectations-augmented) Phillips function has turned out to be rather unstable at certain times, in particular when cost shocks have hit the national economy. For instance, the well-known parallel increase in inflation and unemployment in the mid- and late 1970s (as illustrated by a comparison of figures 2.2 and 2.3) is certainly consistent with the view that it was not mainly expansionary product demand shocks but rather cost shocks that were the basic impulses to inflation at that time. These statistics are also consistent with the rather common view that the cost shocks, and subsequent attempts by

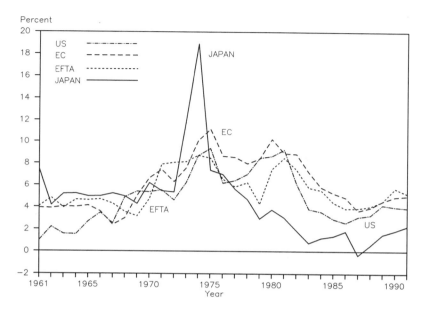

Figure 2.3
Inflation, 1961–1991. Source: OECD *Economic Outlook*, no. 49 (July 1991).
Note: Weights calculated at current gross domestic product (GDP) and 1987
exchange rates. Inflation is defined as the year-to-year percentage change in
GDP deflator.

governments to bring down the inflationary consequences of
these shocks, were crucial factors behind the huge rise in unemployment in that period.

As a rough illustration of demand management policies and
various types of supply shocks in the United States and the EC
countries since the early 1960s, particularly pronounced cost
and demand shocks are schematically marked by arrows in figures 2.4 and 2.5, depicting the path of aggregate employment
and unemployment. (Shocks are classified, rather heuristically,

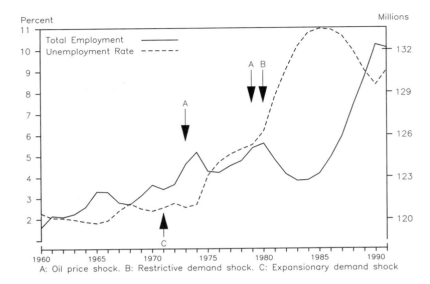

Figure 2.4
Aggregate employment and the unemployment rate in the EC, 1960–1991.
Source: OECD, *Economic Outlook*, no. 49 (July 1991) and previous issues.

on the basis of the charaterization of monetary and fiscal policies in various countries in different issues of the OECD *Economic Outlook*.)

It is a rather common view (consistent with the arrows in figures 2.4 and 2.5) that while supply shocks were relatively important for employment performance in the second half of the 1970s, demand shocks, in the form of restrictive demand management policies, were more important in the 1980s. A comparison of the employment performance in Western Europe and the United States also supports this observation; the fiscal policy stance seems to have been much more expansionary in the

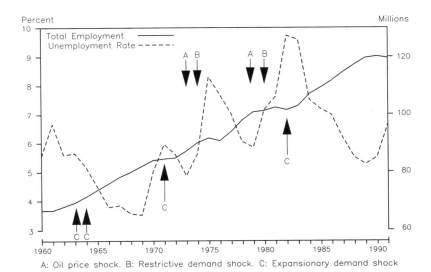

A: Oil price shock. B: Restrictive demand shock. C: Expansionary demand shock

Figure 2.5
Aggregate employment and the unemployment rate in the United States,
1960–1991. Source: OECD, *Economic Outlook*, no. 49 (July 1991) and previous issues.

United States than in Western Europe during the 1980s. (See
OECD *Economic Outlook*, various issues.) Another illustration is
the experience during the period 1985–1990 in the United
Kingdom, where fiscal policy became quite expansionary and
unemployment fell rapidly (Alogoskoufis 1989). Here, then, is
probably an important explanation for the relatively favorable
employment development in the United States in the early
1980s and in the United Kingdom in the late 1980s. These
interpretations of unemployment experiences then assume that
there are systematic transmission mechanisms from aggregate
supply and demand shocks to aggregate output and employ-

ment. To try to clarify these mechanisms is one of the main tasks of this book (in particular in chapters 5 and 6).

Covariance of Changes in Aggregate Employment and the Unemployment Rate

One trivial but important inference from macroeconomic time series is that changes in the unemployment rate, and not just changes in aggregate employment, are important aspects of short- and medium-term macroeconomic developments. Periods of relatively rapid expansion (or contraction) of aggregate employment have usually also been characterized by a considerable fall (or rise) in the unemployment rate. Obvious examples are the development of the unemployment rate in the context of the relatively rapid rise in aggregate employment in the EC area around 1964, 1969, 1973, and 1986–1990, as well as the relatively rapid fall in aggregate employment around 1967, 1975 and 1981–1983 (figure 2.4). The (negative) co-movement between aggregate employment and the unemployment rate is perhaps less obvious in the United States because of the strong long-term upward trend of aggregate employment (figure 2.5). However, the rather strong expansion of aggregate employment in the periods 1963–1969, 1971–1979, and 1984–1989 was connected with quite strong reductions in the unemployment rate. And the leveling off of aggregate employment growth in 1969–1971, 1974–1975, and 1979–1983 was associated with considerable increases in the unemployment rate as will be clear in chapter 6.

For these reasons, an explanation of the movements of the unemployment rate, and not just aggregate employment, is an important aspect of any serious theory of short- and medium-term macroeconomic developments. If unemployment is interpreted as an excess supply of labor and related job rationing, a market-clearing approach to the labor market cannot possibly be appropriate for macroeconomic analysis. The magnitude and persistence of statistically recorded changes in aggregate employment and unemployment are too large to be explained as variations in search or frictional unemployment, intertemporal substitution of leisure, or economic agents misinterpreting inflation as relative price and wage changes in the context of market-clearing models. Moreover, the well-documented unhappiness of many unemployed workers does not suggest that they have simply, in an optimum fashion, reallocated leisure between periods in response to perceived intertemporal wage changes in a labor market with market-clearing wages, as suggested by new classical macroeconomics or real business cycle theories.

This is the background for the goal of this book to deal with aggregate employment and unemployment in the context of a nonclearing labor market. In other words, we have to understand the existence and persistence of a nonmarket-clearing wage; this is the task of the next chapter.

3   The Existence of Unemployment

Generally an individual may be regarded as unemployed if he or she is not only out of work but is available for work and, in fact, seeks work at the prevailing wage (normalized for productivity differences between individuals). The simplest way of representing aggregate unemployment, in the sense of excess supply of labor, is presumably a textbook-type demand-supply diagram for the aggregate labor market with an exogenous (real) product wage rate that is above the potential equilibrium rate and with actual employment determined by the demand side in the labor market.

Where does this nonmarket-clearing wage come from? Until recently, proponents of nonmarket-clearing theories of unemployment had not bothered much about this question, or at least not succeeded very well in answering it. This applies not only to "old" classical macroeconomists, from Hume to Pigou, who admitted temporary situations of excess supply of labor, but also to Keynes and his followers, although neither of these schools provided much of an explanation for assertedly sticky wages. (As an explanation, Keynes sometimes referred to various customary or institutional factors behind prevailing wage rates and on other occasions to concern among employees for relative, rather than real, wages.)

The Barro-Grossman theory of unemployment, with asserted excess supply in both the labor and the product markets, is even more incomplete in the sense that it does not explain how both the aggregate nominal wage rate and the aggregate product price could wind up above the equilibrium level in the respective markets. Nor does this model explain why firms, although they are assumed to be price takers in the product market (perfect competition), nevertheless cannot sell all the goods they would like at the existing product price.

Throughout this book, while the aggregate product market is assumed to clear, the labor market does not, for reasons that will be discussed in some detail. Indeed, when looking at the world around us, it is clear that rationing of jobs is much more prevalent than rationing in the aggregate product market, although there are occasionally both waiting times and "involuntary" changes in inventories for individual products. (A more complete macro model should deal explicitly with inventory fluctuations and perhaps also with variations in delivery times for products.) Such product market clearing is quite consistent with sluggish price responses to aggregate product market shocks.

In order to explain why the labor market does not clear, it is necessary to answer a fundamental question: Why is there so little underbidding of existing wages by unemployed workers? By "underbidding" I mean either that unemployed workers themselves actively try to get jobs by offering to work for less than the prevailing wages of incumbent workers or that firms

successfully offer jobs to unemployed workers at wages below
the existing level.

If such underbidding were to occur, either unemployment
would fall, as claimed by the old classical macroeconomists, or
there may—as sometimes asserted by Keynes—be a limitless
process of deflation of nominal wages and prices without necessarily eliminating unemployment. Because wage underbidding,
with either of these contingencies as a result, does not seem to
be prevalent in the real world, it is important to understand
why this is so.[1] A related analytical task is to explain why
workers who are fired or laid off do not succeed in keeping
their jobs by way of wage cuts—that is, by underbidding the
wages of the remaining incumbent workers.

In trying to answer such questions, this book draws on
and combines several different theories of nonmarket-clearing
wages, with particular attention given to the insider-outsider
theory of unemployment. The reason is not that this theory is
necessarily asserted to be superior to its contenders in explaining the existence of unemployment but rather that it is newer
and less well understood than the others. Therefore, I want to
investigate the potential usefulness of this new approach. The
insider-outsider theory may also be combined with other theories of unemployment; indeed, it helps to fill important analytical gaps in some of these theories.

Alternative Micro-Based Theories of Unemployment

Government Wage Controls

A straightforward, though rather trivial, theory of nonmarket-
clearing wages would consist simply of referring to govern-

ment wage controls. The most obvious example is minimum wage legislation. Such legislation, however, is usually not binding for a very large fraction of wage earners in developed countries. But with pronounced heterogeneity of jobs and workers, government wage regulation can certainly contribute to mismatches between demand and supply in the labor market and, hence, accentuate unemployment of unskilled and handicapped labor, as well as workers in declining geographical regions. Heavy youth unemployment in some countries is a case in point. On balance, it is probably fair to say, however, that minimum wage laws are not a primary explanation behind nonmarket-clearing wages and aggregate unemployment in developed countries. (For instance, the minimum wage in the United States has hovered around 30 percent of the average manufacturing wage.) In particular, minimum wage regulations cannot possibly explain the drastic rise in aggregate unemployment in a number of countries in the mid-1970s and again in the early 1980s.[2]

There are some exceptions. Spain and Portugal, and the eastern part of Germany, are examples among OECD countries; minimum wages there were rather high in the 1970s and 1980s. More pronounced examples are found among less developed countries, particularly in Africa and Latin America.

In countries where minimum wages do provide an important explanation for nonmarket-clearing wages and unemployment, at least for some groups of workers, it would be interesting to answer the political economy question as to why governments actually introduce minimum wage legislation in spite of its unemployment-creating effects. In the analytical tradition in which governments are assumed to function as well-informed and rational social planners, it is natural to regard minimum wage legislation as the outcome of a conscious cost-benefit trade-off by the government. In this case we may think of the government as maximizing a social welfare function with employment and real wages for various groups of workers as arguments, or we may hypothesize that the government is more concerned about the incomes of the working poor than about the situation of those who may become unemployed by way of minimum wage regulations. A more public choice—oriented explanation would emphasize instead the workings of the political process, by arguing, for instance, that political parties compete for votes by offering the electorate minimum wage regulation on the assumption that those who expect to gain income from such regulation can deliver more votes than those who expect to lose their jobs.

However, both the notion of a rational trade-off by the government on the basis of a social welfare function and the pursuit of vote-getting behavior by politicians probably exaggerate the availability of relevant information and the ability of political decision makers to calculate rationally. Ignorance or wishful thinking about the consequences of political actions, and hence the prevalence of various types of political imperfections and economic illusions among politicians, should not be ruled out as an important explanation for political behavior. There may be elements of illusion among the electorate as well. For instance, the positive effects of minimum wage legislation on the incomes of the gainers may be more apparent than the often more indirect negative employment effects on the losers. More bluntly, the role of ignorance in developments in the world should not be underestimated.

Social Norms

Another apparent explanation of nonmarket-clearing wages is
to refer to social norms that make underbidding of wages a
socially unacceptable form of behavior. Metaphorically, there
may exist an implicit Eleventh Commandment telling workers:
"Thou shalt not steal jobs from your fellow workers by underbidding their wages." And there may also be an implicit
Twelfth Commandment telling employers: "Thou shalt not en-
courage, or accept, job theft by way of wage underbidding."
Such social norms certainly exist and may be of great importance, as sociologists would probably testify. However, even
granting that such social norms may help explain the absence of
wage underbidding, a more profound analysis would certainly
make it necessary to look behind these asserted norms and ask
how they emerged, in whose interest they exist, and how they
are upheld. The reason for asking such questions is not only an
ambition to achieve the most comprehensive explanation of the
existence of wage norms. As we shall see, an understanding of
where such norms come from helps explain important aspects
of the functioning of the labor market.

As an attempt to formalize the idea of social norms, Weibull
(1987) and Solow (1990, pp. 38–50) have shown that a Nash
equilibrium may emerge in which unemployed workers abstain
from underbidding in the expectation that they themselves, if
employed in the future, would not be threatened by wage underbidding from others. The Weibull-Solow equilibrium, however, does not explain the incentive mechanisms that make
people abstain from underbidding: an unemployed individual
(in a world with many workers) hardly has an incentive to
abstain from the personal gains associated with successful underbidding on the grounds that his or her own behavior would

create incentives for other individuals to act in a similar fashion in the future (when he or she may have a job).

The problem is rather similar to the voting paradox: the difficulty in explaining why an individual chooses to vote although the probability of his or her influencing the election outcome is negligible. However, whereas in the case of voting we may argue that the cost of voting, too, is negligible, and even that people may actually enjoy the act of voting, we can hardly argue that the costs of not underbidding are negligible. To use another metaphor, it may be surmised that people shovel snow off their sidewalk, expecting their neighbors to do the same. However, this is an example of social control within small groups, in contrast to the Weibull-Solow hypothesis, which refers to large groups of atomistic agents.

It would seem, therefore, that more convincing micro-based disincentives to underbidding behavior have to be identified and explained in the context of theories based on social norms. As it turns out, some versions of both the efficiency wage theory and the insider-outsider theory provide such explanations.

Union Models

These models are so well known that it seems unnecessary to devote much time to presenting them. Formally the union is usually assumed to try to maximize a weighted average of its employed and unemployed members' welfare (utility). If the union is "utilitarian," the weights are the numbers of employed and unemployed members, respectively; the union is, then, concerned with the sum of its members' welfare. On the other hand, if the union's objective is "expected utility," the weights are the proportions of employed and unemployed members,

respectively, to the total membership. According to both for-
mulations, each union member is usually assumed to have an
equal chance of being employed.

Regardless of whether the union sets the wage unilaterally, as
in the union monopoly model, or it is set by way of bargaining
between the union and firms (or an organization of firms), as in
the union bargaining model, it is usually assumed that the firm
decides how much labor to employ at that wage—the so-called
right-to-manage model (Oswald, 1985). The resulting wage-
employment combination, which as a rule will imply some unemployment, is that point on the labor demand curve that
maximizes the union's objective. So-called efficient bargaining,
involving maximization of the union's objective subject to the
firms' achievement of some given level of profit, will for the
most part also generate some unemployment.

An obvious strength of labor union models is that they highlight two potentially important institutional features of labor
markets in the real world (in particular in Western Europe):
labor unions and collective bargaining. Union models also help
explain relative wages and, hence, mismatches between demand
and supply of labor. Accordingly, the varying roles of unions in
different countries probably help explain country differences
not only in the level but also in the structure of unemployment.

Union models have some serious limitations as explanations of
unemployment, however. In particular, they do not emphasize
the reasons that unions are able to push through and sustain
nonmarket-clearing wages; these models do not, by themselves,
explicitly explain where unions get their market power and,
hence, how unions may prevent wage underbidding. More
specifically, why is it that unemployed union members do not

simply leave the union, and why do unorganized unemployed workers not try to obtain, and succeed in getting, jobs by underbidding existing wages?

Adherents of labor union models would probably answer that union threats of collective actions, such as strikes and work-to-rule against deviating firms or workers, will prevent wage underbidding, but this answer merely pushes the question one step back: Why could firms not simply replace striking workers by unemployed workers or workers in the secondary sector of the economy with relatively low wages? One conceivable explanation is that government legislation makes wage contracts, agreed upon in collective bargaining, binding for all employees. This is a valid point, but it cannot explain why underbidding does not occur more often in countries where such legislation does not exist or did not exist before World War I or II.

For these reasons, labor union models are in need of improved microeconomic underpinnings. The insider-outsider theory may help provide such underpinnings.

The limitations of union models as a comprehensive explanation for unemployment in the real world are also revealed by the fact that unemployment often exists in societies with very weak unions or even no unions at all. For instance, it seems far-fetched to refer to union activities when trying to explain periods of high unemployment before World War II, not to speak of the period prior to World War I. Moreover, strong unions did not prevent low unemployment—indeed, full employment—during the 1960s in a number of countries in Western Europe. Nevertheless, union models comprise an important piece in the unemployment puzzle, in particular in combination with other theories, which provide other pieces.

Efficiency Wage Theories

Like labor union models, efficiency wage models do not require any detailed presentation. The essence of various types of efficiency wage theories (Katz 1986) is that firms are willing to pay more than the hypothetical market-clearing wage to recruit good workers, to discourage quitting, or to stimulate employees to work effectively. At a lower wage rate than the prevailing incumbent wage, unemployed workers cannot commit themselves to providing the same amount of labor inputs (measured in efficiency units) as provided by the existing incumbent worker. Problems of adverse selection or moral hazard prevent such commitments. Only by accident would the labor market clear at the wage rate actually chosen by profit-maximizing firms. According to some versions of the efficiency wage theory, unemployment will necessarily prevail at this wage rate because unemployment then serves as a worker's disciplinary device against shirking on the job and quitting. As the importance of efficiency wage mechanisms probably varies between production sectors, the theory also helps explain relative wages and different degrees of excess supply in different sectors of the labor market.

An obvious strength of efficiency wage models is their appeal to common sense and everyday experience, since it is eminently reasonable to assume, as the efficiency wage theory does, that wages are used as a screening device for labor productivity. Thus, like labor union models, efficiency wage models capture an important part of reality by helping to explain the absence of wage underbidding, and hence the existence of unemployment. They also have certain limitations. In particular, workers are assumed to be quite passive in the process of wage setting. The firm is assumed to set the wage unilaterally, and the worker is assumed to react to the firm's wage setting by choosing a job and work effort. This also means that there is no profound role for labor unions in this type of model.

The Insider-Outsider Theory

While in efficiency wage theories it is not in firms' interest to reduce wages, in theories based on insider-outsider mechanisms, it is not in the interest of incumbent workers to do so. The starting point of the insider-outsider theory is that various types of labor turnover costs create "rents" and market power for incumbent workers in existing firms—so-called insiders (Lindbeck and Snower 1984, 1988a). As a result, insiders can push their wages above both the potential market-clearing wage and the reservation wage of workers who are not employed in these firms—so-called outsiders—without the insiders losing their jobs.

Insiders are perceived as experienced incumbent employees whose positions are protected by labor turnover costs; outsiders are either unemployed workers or workers who hold jobs with little job security in the informal (secondary) sector of the economy. In contrast to the descriptive statistical terms "employed" and "unemployed," the terms "insiders" and "outsiders" provide an analytical distinction that highlights the asymmetric position of incumbent workers and unemployed workers (or workers in the secondary sector) in terms of market power, due to the market power of the former.

Perhaps the most obvious type of labor turnover cost is the traditional cost of hiring and firing labor. With respect to hiring, this includes the costs of search, screening, negotiations, and training of newly hired workers. With respect to firing, it includes severance pay and possibly costly firing procedures. While it is a commonplace that direct government intervention in wage formation may create unemployment, the insider-outsider theory highlights the possibility that other interventions, such as job security legislation, through its effects on wage formation, may also be responsible for unemployment.

A second type of labor turnover cost arises because insiders can refuse to cooperate with outsiders who try to get jobs by underbidding the prevailing wages of the insiders. For instance, suppose that an unemployed worker approaches a firm and offers to work for a lower wage than the prevailing insider wage. Insiders may prevent such an attempt at underbidding by threatening not to cooperate with an underbidder in the production process. As a result, the latter's productivity may become so low that it is not in the firm's interest to hire him or her. Insiders may also push up the reservation wage of outsiders by threatening to harass those who try to break into the firm through wage underbidding. Because such threats of noncooperation and harassment activities may make underbidding either unprofitable for firms or disagreeable for the underbidders themselves, we have a supplementary explanation for the absence of underbidding by unemployed workers.

Although traditional hiring and firing costs, including severance payments, occur only once, turnover costs that are associated with threats of noncooperation and harassment activities may create expected costs to firms in every period during which an underbidder is employed, provided that the threats are credible. This tends to make the latter type of turnover costs quantitatively more important than the former.

Because the subsequent exposition will rely on insider-outsider mechanisms to a considerable extent, it is useful to highlight the basic idea of the theory using a simple formalization.[3] To simplify the discussion, the individual firm is assumed to make decisions about wages and employment in two steps. First, the nominal wage is assumed to be determined, most realistically, through bargaining. In the second step, each firm makes its output and employment decisions (and in the case of imperfect competition also pricing decisions), taking the nominal wage as given.

The basic model is depicted in Figure 3.1. In the upper part of the figure, referring to an individual firm, the product wage is shown on the vertical axis (w_I for insiders and w_E for entrants); the input of labor—of insiders (L_I) and entrants (L_E)—is represented on the horizontal axis. The production function of the firm is $f(L_I + L_E)$. (In a more general formulation, we may assume that insiders are more productive than outsiders.) IDC (insider demand curve) denotes the demand curve for insiders. It is easy to show, and equally easy to understand intuitively, that the IDC curve is determined as the marginal product of labor (f') plus the marginal costs (F') of firing labor. In a similar way, EDC (entrance demand curve) denotes the demand curve for entrants, which is equal to the marginal product minus the marginal costs of hiring workers: $f' - H'$ (Lindbeck and Snower 1988a). Thus, the traditional labor demand curve—that is, the marginal product curve, when there are no specific labor turnover costs—lies somewhere between the IDC and the EDC curves, for instance, as illustrated by the broken curve (denoted MP).

If the product price is given for the individual firm (perfect competition in the product market), the product wage may also be interpreted as the nominal wage. The labor demand relation looks very much the same if we instead assume imperfect com-

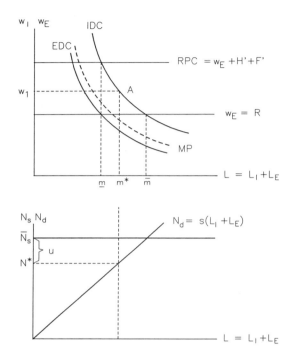

Figure 3.1
Employment determination in the insider-outsider theory

petition in the product market, although then the curve is not a "proper" demand curve but an optimum relation between the real wage rate and the employment level of the firm (see chapter 6).

Let us now assume that the wages for entrants are equal to their reservation wage (R): $w_E = R$. This entrant wage is depicted by a horizontal line in the figure. One line in the figure remains to be explained, the horizontal line RPC, which shows the relative profitability constraint or, intuitively, the maximum wage that insiders may obtain without being replaced by outsiders. This maximum wage is equal to the entrant wage plus the sum of the marginal costs of hiring and firing labor ($w_E + H' + F'$): if the insider wage is higher than that, it pays for the firm to replace insiders by outsiders. (The vertical distance between the w_E line and the RPC line is then ($H' + F'$).)

So far the figure has been explained in terms of the hiring-firing version of the insider-outsider theory. However, it may alternatively be interpreted in terms of the noncooperation-harassment version. In this case, the difference between the IDC and the EDC curves depends on the fact that insiders may keep down the productivity of entrants if the latter try to underbid existing wages; moreover, by harassing the underbidders, insiders may push up the reservation wage of outsiders and hence also the entrant wage.

Assume that the number of insiders inherited from the previous period is m^*. Let us also look at the simple case where insiders have complete market power in the sense that they may acquire the entire rent generated in connection with the marginal turnover costs.[4] Insiders are therefore able to push up their wage rate to w_1, that is, to point A. All insiders will then keep their jobs, but no entrants will be admitted because their marginal productivity after deducting for labor turnover costs is below the entrant wage. If there are unemployed workers in this situation, they will remain unemployed as long as the EDC curve and the entrant wage do not change. If instead the number of (inherited) insiders is initially smaller than $\underline{m}$, the firm will hire more workers ("hiring scenario"), and if the number is greater than $\overline{m}$, some insiders will be fired even if they would accept an entrant wage ("firing scenario"). An initial (inherited) employment level between $\underline{m}$ and $\overline{m}$ implies that the number of employees is unchanged ("retention scenario").

On an aggregate level of analysis, the consequences for labor demand depend on the distribution of firms among various scenarios. However, in order to explain in the simplest way how unemployment can arise in the insider-outsider model, let us assume that there is a given number, say s, of identical firms, so that the total demand for labor is $L_d = s \cdot (L_I + L_E)$. At the labor demand m^* of the individual firm, aggregate labor demand, N^*, may then simply be read off along the line N_d in the lower part of figure 3.1. If aggregate labor supply is assumed to be given at $\overline{N}_s$, then unemployment is u.[5]

Assuming that labor turnover costs vary among production sectors and among different types of workers, the insider-outsider theory also helps explain the relative wage structure, and hence also the distribution of unemployment over different sectors, in the context of a heterogeneous labor market.

There are some problems with the insider-outsider theory. One is that wages are sometimes not public information, especially in nonunion sectors (for example, in some services). The noncooperation-harassment version of the insider-outsider theory may not be relevant in such cases because insiders may not know when to retaliate against underbidders. In large sectors of the economy, however, it is likely that both insiders and outsiders have a reasonably accurate idea of going wage rates, at least for unskilled workers, who bear the heaviest burden of unemployment.

Another potential reservation to the insider-outsider theory is that new firms, which by definition have no insiders, may hire unemployed workers at their reservation wage and undersell established firms, particularly perhaps in the case of large, persistent unemployment. Thus, the role of entry of firms in wage formation has to be taken into consideration.

One particularly simple type of entry is to become self-employed. Whoever cannot work for someone else could work for himself or herself. In principle, it is probably always possible to find some form of self-employment. As extreme examples, most people have the option of becoming street peddlers or selling flowers from an improvised stand somewhere. Still, a schoolteacher or a skilled (white- or blue-collar) worker who, after having lost his or her job, prefers leisure to selling flowers or newspapers on the street would, most likely, be classified as involuntarily unemployed. In other words, self-employment in the secondary (informal) sector of the economy is limited because the reservation wage of the worker may be higher than the utility received from such work. This issue is considered later in the context of the secondary labor market.

There may also be more specific obstacles to the entry of firms, such as risk aversion, limited entrepreneurial skills, and limitations of equity capital and borrowed funds (credit rationing). This means that although entry of firms may be an important potential factor in undercutting the power of insiders, such entry probably cannot eliminate unemployment, or at least it may take a very long time for the entry of firms to bring this about. This tendency is accentuated by the fact that legislation in some countries makes collective bargaining agreements binding for established firms as well as new firms.

A third problem with the insider-outsider theory is that a firm that wants insiders to accept lower wages (say following a reduction in product demand) could pit the insiders in one plant against those in another plant. It could offer the following alternatives: the plant, and its insiders, that settle for the lower wage will remain open; the other will be shut down. Insiders in this case encounter a "profitability constraint" (they hit the RPC line in figure 3.1): a plant is closed down, as being unprofitable, if insiders insist on keeping their wages. Rational insiders in this example may prefer wage reductions. (A centralized union operating above the level of individual plants owned by a firm, and perhaps also above individual firms, might be able to prevent such wage concessions.)

Relations between Theories

Theories of government wage controls, labor union behavior, efficiency wages, social norms, and insider-outsider mechanisms should be regarded as complementary, not competing, theories. It is worth noting, however, that both the insider-outsider theory and the efficiency wage theory explain the absence of wage underbidding, and hence the existence of unemployment, without having to refer to either government wage controls or labor unions. Thus, the insider-outsider theory is not, as some commentators have asserted, a variation of labor union models. Unlike the efficiency wage theory, however, the insider-outsider theory establishes a rationale for unions.

In particular, unions may both raise the turnover costs of labor and help workers exploit existing turnover costs in the bargaining process more efficiently than workers who bargain individually. For instance, unions may raise hiring and firing costs either by bargaining with firms over such costs or by lobbying politically for legislation with the same implications. Labor turnover costs also give clout to union threats of strikes and work-to-rule activities, which helps insiders to acquire a larger fraction of the value added than otherwise. Unions may also organize noncooperation and harassment activities within firms more effectively than individual workers operating without a formal organization; noncooperation and harassment activities are basically collective actions, even if they do not necessarily require any formal organization such as a union.

As the insider-outsider theory helps explain where the market power of unions comes from, it contributes to filling an analytical gap in union models, regardless of whether they are union monopoly models or (more realistically) union bargaining models. Indeed, the insider-outsider theory may be said to help explain the existence of unemployment and labor unions simultaneously.

Efficiency wage and insider-outsider mechanisms are complements in the sense that they may be combined in one model. For instance, if efficiency wage mechanisms are added to an insider-outsider model, the (quasi)equilibrium wage rate would be predicted to rise because marginal profits will now be higher than before for a given wage rate (if the elasticity of labor productivity with respect to the wage is initially greater than unity). However, in a model that already includes both insider-outsider and efficiency wage mechanisms and the firm has adjusted optimally, the two mechanisms tend, on the margin, to weaken rather than strengthen each other. The intuitive reason is that the greater the market power of unions is, the smaller is the need for the firm to raise the wage rate for efficiency wage reasons, and vice versa (see Lindbeck and Snower 1991a for a formal analysis).

Union models, efficiency wage models, and insider-outsider models are usually built on the notion of rational economic optimization. However, it is important to realize that much of human behavior is based on habits and social norms. This aspect has in fact been considered in some versions of both the efficiency wage and the insider-outsider theories. In Akerlof's (1982) version of the efficiency wage theory, it is assumed that the efficiency of work is largely a result of social norms among employees and that these norms are based on an exchange of "gifts" between firms and their employees. Firms "give away" wage payments in addition to the reservation wage of workers and the potential market equilibrium wage, whereas workers give the firm a pro quo gift in exchange, in the form of extra work effort.

The noncooperation and harassment version of the insider-outsider theory also helps explain the emergence and sustainability of social norms against underbidding. More specifically, the ability of insiders to pursue noncooperation and harassment activities helps provide them with the market power required to create and sustain social norms against underbidding. Thus, such norms are created in the interest of insiders and are upheld by threats of noncooperation and harassment toward underbidders. These norms are also supported by derogatory terms, such as scabs, for underbidders. Whereas Akerlof's version of the efficiency wage theory is built on assumed norms among employed workers concerning wages and work effort, the noncooperation-harassment version of the insider-outsider theory establishes wage norms also among unemployed workers. Indeed, the history after the industrial revolution shows that insiders sometimes treated underbidders quite harshly, even beating them up, which over the years has helped create norms against underbidding. Once such norms become well established, fewer threats have to be exercised against potentially underbidding outsiders.

The insider-outsider theory may also help explain the emergence of government wage controls, such as minimum wage legislation. Minimum wage legislation is often in the interest of insiders, as outsiders will then be legally prevented from engaging in wage underbidding. However, since explicit minimum wages are often quite low as compared to insider wages, legislation that instead makes it illegal for firms to pay wages below those agreed upon in collective bargaining, also for nonorganized workers and for new firms, is probably a more important type of de facto minimum wage legislation than minimum wage legislation itself. Indeed, in several countries, legislation against wages below those agreed upon in collective bargaining may be the proximate reason that firms and unemployed workers do not engage in underbidding the prevailing wages of incumbent workers.

The Involuntariness of Unemployment

Is it reasonable to regard the type of unemployment covered by the theories discussed as involuntary? This question cannot be answered until we have defined involuntary unemployment. Two alternatives, proposed in Lindbeck and Snower (1988, pp. 47–52) and Lindbeck (1992), may be worth considering in this context:

Definition 1: At prevailing current wages and future expected wages, some workers are unsuccessful in finding jobs because, at no fault of their own, they face a more limited choice set between work and leisure than employed workers, even if the wage demands of the former are adjusted for productivity differences, including unavoidable (production-related) resource costs in connection with hiring and firing of workers.

Definition 2: Some workers are unable to get jobs even though their reservation wage is lower than the value of their marginal product, adjusted for unavoidable (production-related) resource costs.

Definition 2 is obviously narrower than definition 1. If unemployed workers seek jobs at wages that are lower than their marginal product but are unable to find such work, then according to definition 2, these workers must have a more limited choice set than current jobholders with the same characteristics. This means that definition 2 is included in definition 1. On the other hand, definition 1 does not necessarily imply definition 2. Given the more limited choice set of the unemployed workers, their reservation wage may very well be higher than their marginal product—for instance, as a result of the discrimination to which unemployed workers may be exposed.

Unemployment is involuntary in efficiency wage models in terms of both definitions 1 and 2. Unemployed workers, in line with definition 1, have a more limited choice set than employed workers; unemployed workers cannot commit themselves to the same work effort as employed workers at a lower wage rate than the current one. Moreover, in line with definition 2, the reservation wage of unemployed workers may very well be lower than their potential marginal product, in a hypothetical case in which unemployed workers actually have the same job opportunities as currently employed workers.

In union models in which union preferences perfectly reflect member preferences and all union members are equal and have the same chance of getting a job, it may be argued instead that the ensuing unemployment level is "chosen voluntarily" and then perhaps not worth worrying about. In the real world, however, individual workers' chances of getting a job differ (also among workers with equal skills), depending on whether a worker is employed initially. In such cases, it is more realistic to use types of union models in which union members differ and are not treated equally: currently unemployed workers' chances of having a job in the next period are assumed to be smaller than those of employed workers. The ensuing unemployment, by definition 1 as well as 2, may then be characterized as '"union-voluntary but member-involuntary unemployment" (Corden 1981). This holds for both monopoly union models and union bargaining models; however, in the case of union bargaining models, the wage rate would normally be expected to be lower, and the employment level higher, than in union monopoly models. As a result, unemployment would be expected to be lower in union bargaining models than in union monopoly models.

Is unemployment also involuntary according to the insider-outsider theory? In some respects, such a characterization is quite reasonable: the unemployed are denied work even if they would accept a job at the same wage as (or even a lower wage than) incumbent workers (with deduction of unavoidable, production-related resource costs associated with hiring and training labor). Outsiders would like to be in the insiders' shoes but are denied that opportunity.

The sense in which workers could be regarded as "involuntarily" unemployed (by definition 1) may be highlighted metaphorically in the context of the insider-outsider theory. Suppose that a woman is confronted by a mugger on a street corner. He offers her a choice: "your money or your life." She hands over her purse, hence choosing her life. Some hard-boiled observer might say that this is voluntary behavior since she did have a choice between her purse and her life. However, most people would probably agree that this is a clear-cut instance of involuntary behavior, since the woman was exposed to an exceptionally narrow choice set. It is this discrimination, embodied in an artificially narrowed choice set, that constitutes involuntariness for the woman.

The involuntariness of unemployment in the insider-outsider theory is of a similar nature. By no fault of their own, outsiders are exposed to social discrimination as compared to those who already have a job, and therefore they have a smaller choice set than incumbent workers, in addition to what can be explained by differences in intrinsic productivity. In this sense, we can talk about involuntariness regardless of whether the turnover costs of labor are caused by legislated costs of firing labor or whether they are related to threats of noncooperation-harassment activities on the part of insiders.

This notion of the involuntariness of unemployment in the insider-outsider theory probably captures what laypeople consider to be its most distinguishing feature: the social injustice of being unemployed due to discriminatory job rationing associated with the unequal opportunities caused by social factors rather than by intrinsic differences between individuals.

Thus, in the context of the insider-outsider theory, unemployment may reasonably be regarded as involuntary by definition 1. But according to definition 2, unemployment is not involuntary in the context of the hiring-firing version of the insider-outsider theory, if the entrant wage coincides with the reservation wage of outsiders (entrants). The reservation wage in this case is higher than the marginal product of labor after deduction of hiring costs, which are basically production-related resource costs (figure 3.1). By contrast, we may certainly speak of involuntariness if insiders, for instance, through bargaining, have pushed up the entrant wage above both the reservation wage of outsiders and the marginal product of entrants (exclusive of unavoidable hiring costs).

In the context of the noncooperation-harassment version of the insider-outsider theory, however, it is also reasonable to talk about involuntary unemployment according to the alternative definition of involuntariness (definition 2). Outsiders are denied work in spite of the fact that their marginal product would have been higher than their reservation wage, provided insiders had not pushed down the (expected) productivity of entrants with threats of noncooperation, pushed up their reservation wage with threats of harassment, or both.

One conceivable objection to this way of analyzing unemployment may be that there would, in principle, be an entrant wage low enough for outsiders to be hired, regardless of the size of labor turnover costs. The higher the turnover costs are, and hence also the wage that a worker can expect to receive in the future when he or she becomes an insider, the lower is the wage a newly employed worker should be willing to accept today as an entrant wage. From this point of view, it may be tempting to argue that the insider-outsider theory does not really explain unemployment but merely the steepness of the intertemporal wage profile.

In my view, however, this is not a realistic way of perceiving the issue, for several reasons. First, an increase in the insider wage may easily raise the present value of the firm's expected long-term wage costs per entrant, and hence discourage new hiring, even if a higher expected insider wage in the future would make entrants more willing to make wage concessions today. For example, workers may have a shorter time horizon than firms when considering the consequences of expected future wages. More specifically, if workers have a higher rate of time discount than firms, a rise in the insider wage may not reduce the reservation wage of entrants sufficiently to prevent the firm's present value of wage costs (under the firm's rate of time discount) from rising. Second, the wage at which the firm would be willing to hire a worker may exceed the entrant's reservation wage because that wage would be unfeasible for the entrant on account of credit restrictions or minimum wage laws. There is also a moral hazard problem here: the firm may have an incentive to fire entrants before they become insiders if the entrant wage is equal to the true reservation wage. Moreover, the insiders (possibly operating through their unions) may directly (for instance, through bargaining) exert upward pressure on the entrant wage in order to discourage underbidding.

The literature contains several suggestions for constructing ingenious labor contracts aimed at eliminating involuntary unemployment, in the context of both insider-outsider and efficiency wage theories. The background is that involuntary unemployment is Pareto inefficient, so that there are unexploited gains from trade among firms, incumbent employees, and unemployed workers. It turns out, however, that such contracts are difficult to construct and implement. (For a detailed discussion of this issue in the context of the insider-outsider theory, see Lindbeck 1992.)

There are also some philosophical problems inherent in the idea of involuntary economic behavior, including assertedly involuntary unemployment. For instance, some vacancies always exist simultaneously with unemployment, and the intensity of search for suitable vacancies by unemployed workers is an aspect that each individual worker decides on his or her own and that influences this person's probability of getting a job. In this sense, there is an element of voluntariness in being unemployed for those who could get jobs through more intensive search. Moreover, there are always some low-wage jobs available in the informal, or secondary, sector of the economy, for workers who do not get jobs in the primary sector. In the context of the efficiency wage theory, the secondary sector may be defined in terms of the relative unimportance of efficiency wage effects in that sector, whereas in the context of the insider-outsider theory, it may be defined in terms of low labor turnover costs and/or weak unions and, hence, weak insider market power. Indeed, for the secondary sector, it may—as an approximation —be reasonable to treat the existing wage rate as a market-clearing wage.

All of this means that we should try to explain not only why some workers are involuntarily shut out from the primary sector of the economy but also why they choose unemployment rather than being employed in the secondary sector. We do have theories that attempt to explain the division of workers into open unemployment and secondary sector work. The most realistic approach, in my opinion, is to refer to the heterogeneity of labor in terms of preferences, productivity, or wealth. In that context, the alternative income of an individual who is not working—unemployment benefits and family income support —also becomes important in explaining why a worker is unemployed. This is not a very profound explanation. It becomes somewhat more interesting if it is assumed that these differences among individual workers are not exogenous phenomena but change endogenously in response to previous work and unemployment experience (Lindbeck and Snower 1990b). For instance, workers who have lost their jobs in the primary sector may be more reluctant than secondary sector workers to take jobs in that sector; they may have the wrong skills for work in that sector; or they may have accumulated some wealth that enables them to afford open unemployment for some period of time.

By adding a secondary labor market to this analysis, a characteristic feature of an unemployed worker would be that while his or her reservation wage is below the actual wage rate of insiders (for workers with similar skills) in the primary sector, it is above the wage rate that he or she would obtain in the secondary, market-clearing sector. Unemployed workers cannot escape job discrimination in the primary sector simply by accepting a job in the secondary sector. It is perhaps due to considerations such as these that work at some low-paid jobs, with very little job security for the individual in the secondary sector, is often called "disguised unemployment."

Indeed, in societies where legislation gives incumbent workers particularly good job security, we may also expect a secondary labor market to emerge within firms operating in the primary sector of the economy. More specifically, we would predict the recourse of employers to temporary workers—those with job contracts (or informal job agreements) for only a limited (fixed) period. Such development has, in fact, recently occurred on a large scale in countries as dissimilar in other respects as Spain and Sweden, probably as a result of very high job security for ordinary workers.

4   The Macroeconomic Framework

Chapter 3 suggested several promising hypotheses for explaining the existence of nonmarket-clearing wages and hence unemployment in the sense of excess supply of labor and related job rationing. But nothing was said about the possibility that the nonmarket-clearing wage itself is systematically influenced by the size of aggregate unemployment. According to reasonably sophisticated versions of the various theories of nonmarket-clearing wages, this would be expected to be the case.

In the context of union and insider-outsider theories, it is less "dangerous" for employees in individual firms to push up wages when the aggregate unemployment rate is low than when it is high, because the probability of being reemployed after losing one's job is relatively high in the former case. And in the context of various efficiency wage theories, a lower aggregate unemployment rate accentuates the need for firms to offer high wage rates to limit shirking and quitting, to get a high-quality selection of work applicants, or both.

This intuitive reasoning suggests a positive relation between aggregate employment, at given labor supply, and wage setting. Following a rather generally accepted terminology, this relation will be called a wage setting function.[1] However, such a positive relation cannot be derived unambiguously from all versions of union models, insider-outsider models, and efficiency wage models. Cases do exist in which the wage setting curve, in real wage and aggregate employment space, is horizontal or vertical, or even downward sloping. As the normal case, however, I assume that the wage setting curve is upward sloping in real wage and aggregate employment space (at given labor supply), although the possibilities of a horizontal wage setting curve in the very short run and a vertical wage setting curve in the very long run will also be discussed.[2] (In models in which an exogenous nonmarket-clearing wage is assumed, we may say that a horizontal wage setting curve is implied.)

Instead of rigorously deriving a wage setting function from one specific micro-based version of union models, efficiency wage models, or insider-outsider models—derivations that have already appeared in the literature—I postulate a typical wage setting function for this set of theories. Let the (real) product wage that is generated by the wage setting process be a rising function of the ratio between aggregate employment, N, and the labor force, $\overline{N}$. In most versions of the wage setting theories already discussed, the product wage rate is also an increasing function of the size of the unemployment benefits in real terms, B. In the context of union and insider-outsider models, the intuition is that higher unemployment benefits tend to raise the reservation wage of workers and to reduce the disadvantages for incumbent workers of being priced out of their present jobs. In the context of efficiency wage models, increased unemployment benefits mean that firms have to pay higher wages than before to recruit workers and to discourage quitting and shirking.

Wage setting is also assumed to be a positive function of labor productivity, represented here by the productivity parameter b, as suggested by both the insider-outsider theory and other theories according to which workers share rents with firms. The wage setting function, then, simply reads

$$w = G(N/\bar{N}, \; b, \; B). \quad \text{(WS function)} \tag{4.1}$$
$${}_{(+)} \phantom{/\bar{N},} {}_{(+)} {}_{(+)}$$

In equation 4.1, the influence of factors inside the firm on wage setting is reflected in the productivity variable b, which is relevant, in particular, for union models and insider-outsider models. In the context of an insider-outsider framework, the role of factors outside the firm, such as the aggregate (un)employment rate and the level of unemployment benefits, reflects the fact that this is not a pure insider theory but literally an insider-outsider theory. Thus, it should not (as some researchers have implied) be tested by looking at the relative importance of factors inside and outside the firm, respectively, for wage setting, even if this issue certainly is of interest in itself. Outside factors will influence wage setting behavior even if incumbent workers care only about themselves, hence neglecting the welfare of outsiders. The reason is that the wage setting ambitions of insiders are influenced by the situation they encounter if they lose their jobs.

It has become increasingly common in macroeconomics to model the determination of real wages and aggregate employment as the outcome of the interplay of an aggregate wage setting function of this general type with an aggregate labor demand function, each expressed in real terms. Assuming imperfect competition in the product market, the latter function is obviously not a strict labor demand curve but rather an optimum relation for firms between the real wage and the employment level. To avoid misunderstandings, I call the curve a labor demand relation rather than a labor demand curve.

Assuming that aggregation over firms generates a macroeconomic labor demand relation of the same basic form as a standard microeconomic labor demand relation, it may simply be written:

$$N_d = C(\underset{(-)\,(+)\,(-)}{w,\ b,\ m}), \tag{4.2}$$

where the parameter m denotes Lerner's measure of monopoly power of a representative firm. The function is illustrated by the LD curve in Figure 4.1a, where the wage setting function (WS) is also depicted. (The signs of the partial derivates are obvious from traditional microeconomic theory.)

For convenience, let us also write the inverse of function 4.2,

$$w_d = D(\underset{(-)\,(+)\,(-)}{N,\ b,\ m}), \qquad \text{(LD function)} \tag{4.2a}$$

where w_d denotes the real wage demanded by the firm for alternative levels of labor inputs.

Aggregate employment (N) and the real wage (w) are then determined by the condition

$$w = w_d, \tag{4.3}$$

implying that N is solved out from

$$G(N/\overline{N}, b, B) = D(N, b, m), \tag{4.3a}$$

that is, $N = g(b, B, m, \overline{N})$; w may then be solved out from equation 4.1 or 4.2a.

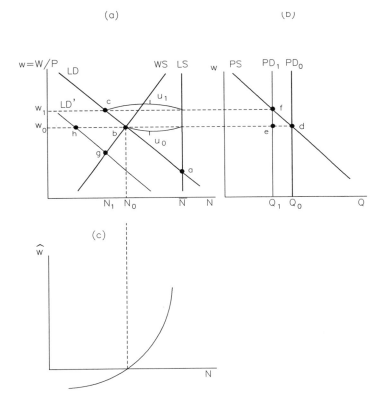

Figure 4.1
Determination of unemployment and output

The solution is depicted by point b in figure 4.1, at the intersection of the LD and WS curves rather than at point a, as in market-clearing models. For simplicity of diagrammatic exposition, it is assumed that labor supply (LS) is vertical, an assumption that may be defended by the lack of solid empirical knowledge about the relative strength of the income and substitution effects of changes in the real wage rate on aggregate labor supply. (The principles of the analysis do not change if the labor supply curve would instead be somewhat upward or downward sloping.) Unemployment is u_0. In the context of a model with a secondary sector, u_0 should be interpreted as open unemployment plus secondary sector employment.

The level of unemployment in the real world would be expected to depend also on the structure of the labor market, including factors such as the choosiness of employers, as well as mismatches between demand and supply of labor among production sectors, occupations, skills, regions, and so forth. All these features are presumably reflected in the relation between vacancies and unemployment, as usually depicted by the UV curve (the Beveridge curve). While such mismatches are probably important explanations of statistically measured levels of unemployment at a given point in time, attempts to explain the increase in unemployment in various countries between the mid-1970s and mid-1980s by more pronounced mismatches have not been successful (see, for instance, Layard, Nickell, and Jackman 1991.).

This general type of organizational framework for macroeconomic analysis of the labor market is shared today by adherents of several different theories of wage setting behavior—union theories (Layard and Nickell 1986; Calmfors 1990), efficiency wage theories (Shapiro and Stiglitz 1984), and insider-outsider

theories (Lindbeck and Snower 1990a)—although the specification of the functions of the model differs considerably among
authors. I call this type of model the LD-WS model of real wage
and aggregate employment determination. Position b is called
the *quasi-equilibrium rate of unemployment (QERU)*—"equilibrium" because the point is a solution to equations 4.1 through
4.3, and "quasi" because there is aggregate excess supply of
labor.[3] Such a quasi-equilibrium position is the only point at
which the demand for labor is consistent with real wage setting
behavior. The WS and LD curves are not necessarily independent of each other in all variants of these types of theories. In
the context of the model presented, the productivity parameter,
b, is an argument in both the wage setting function and the
labor demand relation. (In union monopoly models, the wage
setting curve represents the expansion path, for different levels
of the labor demand curve; the slope of the wage setting curve
depends in this case on how shifts of the labor demand curve
influence the elasticity of that curve.)

Some clarification of the term "real wage setting" may be in
order. No single agent actually sets the real wage. Rather, we
may say that the WS curve defines the setting of nominal
wages, given product prices, and that the LD curve defines the
nominal prices that are set by firms for alternative labor inputs,
given nominal wages. In Layard and Nickell's (1986) useful
terminology, in the context of a somewhat similar framework,
we may say that the WS curve describes the markup of wages
over prices and the LD curve the markup of prices over wages
and that the intersection of the curves defines the level of unemployment for which these markups are consistent.

A characteristic feature of this organizational framework is the
distinction between *labor supply*, which is provided by indi-

vidual households, and *wage setting*, which is performed by firms, insiders, unions, or the process of collective bargaining, depending on which specific theory of wage setting is entertained. This analytical framework has three important advantages as compared to macromodels in which the labor market clears, such as new classical macroeconomics and real business cycle models. First, it allows explicit determination of unemployment, in the sense of excess supply of labor, and not just aggregate employment. Second, the model deals explicitly with wage and price setting behavior, which means that we can retire the mythical auctioneer in both the product and the labor market. Finally, the magnitude of changes in aggregate employment in response to demand and supply shocks in this framework is not closely tied to the elasticity of the labor supply function, by contrast to market-clearing models. This is advantageous because explanations of large fluctuations in aggregate employment do not have to rely on the dubious assumption of a highly elastic supply of labor by the household sector; what matters is the elasticity of the wage setting curve.

This analytical framework is quite different from models that assume monopolistic competition in the labor market (Hart 1982; Bénassy 1976; Blanchard and Kiyotaki 1987). In the latter type of model, the labor supply curve is indistinguishable from the wage setting curve in the same way as the price setting curve and the product supply curve of firms are indistinguishable when firms operate under monopolistic competition in the product market. The reason is that labor supply and wage setting in that type of model are decided simultaneously by the same agent, whom we may call a "syndicate" of workers that control the supply of labor, by contrast to the analysis above where the wage is set by one agent (or by a process, such as collective bargaining), while labor is supplied by other agents (households).

In models with monopolistic competition in the labor market, it is rather meaningless to talk about unemployment because the suppliers of labor themselves choose the desired combination of wages and employment. Thus, there is no excess supply of labor in such models, although the situation is Pareto inefficient ("underemployment equilibrium") due to the absence of perfect competition in the labor market and perhaps also the product market. This illustrates the importance of making a clear distinction between suboptimal aggregate employment, on one hand, and unemployment in the sense of excess supply of labor and related job rationing, on the other.

Models of monopolistic competition in the labor market are analytically equivalent to the union monopoly model in which all workers are union members, and the union maximizes the expected utility of identical members, each with the same probability of being unemployed. The union is assumed to behave as if all employee households had given it the right to supply labor services on their behalf, like a syndicate of workers. Analogously, if members of assumed syndicates of workers are heterogeneous in terms of preferences but the syndicate nevertheless decides wage rates that do not represent the income-leisure trade-off of all members of the syndicate, the model converges to union models in which some members are involuntarily unemployed.

Although it is a useful organizational framework, the LD-WS model is unfinished business as a foundation for macroeconomic analysis. Three extensions and modifications of the model will make it more useful for the subsequent analysis. First, in order to analyze the effects of product demand shocks, including monetary shocks, it is necessary to introduce the demand side in the product market more explicitly and, in this connection, also determine the price level and specify nominal wage and price dynamics. Second, it is important to modify the model to make it consistent with the empirical observation that there seems to be no long-term trendwise relation between the size of the labor force ($\overline{N}$) and the level of labor productivity (b) on one hand and the unemployment rate on the other hand (as mentioned in chapter 2). Third, and most important, it is necessary to introduce mechanisms of unemployment persistence, which will be analyzed here as the dependence of the LD or WS curves on the previous development of aggregate employment or unemployment.

The LD-WS model is derived from first principles in the sense that it is based on microeconomic theories of profit-maximizing firms and utility-maximizing workers and/or unions, although some nontraditional constraints such as efficiency wage mechanisms or insider-outsider mechanisms of wage formation have been added to the traditional analysis. However, the stability of the LD and WS functions over time may certainly be questioned, as may the possibilities of estimating them statistically without serious bias. For instance, wage setting behavior is most likely influenced by changes in the economic policy regime, such as changes in the degree to which government pursues accommodating policies. Thus, econometric estimations of this analytical framework are certainly vulnerable to the Lucas critique. Indeed, it is not obvious that a simple model such as this should be exposed to econometric estimation at all. Perhaps its main usefulness is to provide a general framework for thinking and discussions rather than for quantifications. Attempts have nevertheless been made to estimate wage setting functions of this type (Layard, Nickell, and Jackman 1991, ch. 9; Calmfors and Forslund 1990; Calmfors and Nymoen 1990).

Before specifying the demand side in the product market, it may be noted that a product supply function is implicit in the labor demand relation and that it has the same properties. Hence, the aggregate product supply function may be written

$$Q = Q(N, b) = \underset{(-)(+)(-)}{J(w,\ b,\ m)}. \qquad \text{(PS function)} \qquad (4.4)$$

As an illustration, figure 4.1 is extended by another quadrant, where the aggregate product market is also depicted. The equilibrium aggregate output level (Q_0) is then read off at point d in figure 4.1b on the product supply curve (PS), after the real wage (w_0) has been determined in the labor market subset.

It remains to specify the product demand function, for the purpose of determining equilibrium in the aggregate product market and the aggregate price level. The aggregate demand function is quite conventional and contains four variables. First, there are two monetary variables: real money balances (M/P) and the real exchange rate ($e \cdot P^*/P$), where M is the money stock, P and P^* the product price of domestically and foreign produced goods, respectively, and e the exchange rate. Empirical analysis and experience from various countries suggest that the effects of changes in the price level on aggregate demand for domestic output are much stronger by the real exchange rate (that is, by way of overvalued or undervalued exchange rates) than by the real value of money balances.

Assuming that employed workers are constrained in their hours of work, the product demand function will also include as arguments real aggregate labor income, $w \cdot N$, and profits, $Q - w \cdot N$

(Lindbeck 1963, pp. 33–34, 42–44; Clower 1965). However, I do not intend to emphasize the role of redistributions of national income between labor and capital. These types of income will therefore be introduced into the product demand functions as an aggregate, Q. A real shift parameter (A) is also assumed to enter the aggregate product demand function (PD function), which then reads

$$Q_d = K(M/P, e \cdot P^*/P, Q, A), \quad \text{(PD function)} \quad (4.5)$$
$${(+)} \quad {(+)} \quad {(+)}\ {(+)}$$

and which is depicted in figure 4.1b.[4] If Q had instead been replaced by separate arguments for aggregate labor income ($w \cdot N$) and profits ($Q - w \cdot N$), the PD curve in figure 4.1b would not, in general, have been vertical; this would not, however, change the principles of the subsequent analysis.[5]

The usefulness of the model could certainly be improved by explicitly introducing capital formation, as well as debt-equity considerations of firms and credit rationing, and allowing such factors to influence demand and supply of products and labor. In particular, if firms are concerned about their debt positions ("reluctance toward debt") and if rationing occurs in capital markets, changes in the cash flow and in the net wealth position of firms will influence investment and production decisions (Lindbeck 1963, ch. 3, 4; Greenwald and Stiglitz 1988). In the present model, we may vaguely let changes in M also reflect such considerations.

Assuming that the aggregate product market clears in the sense that there is no (formal or informal) rationing of either buyers or sellers in the product market, the equilibrium requirement for the product market determines P after w, N, and hence also Q, have been determined in the labor market,[6]

$$Q_D = Q, \qquad\qquad\qquad\qquad (4.6)$$

that is,

$$K(M/P, e \cdot P^*/P, Q, A) = J(w, b, m). \qquad\qquad (4.6a)$$

when M, e, and P^* are given.

The nominal wage rate is then determined as $W = w \cdot P$.

The extended LD-WS model outlined so far adheres to the traditional dichotomy between the determination of real and nominal variables, and related neutrality of money, although the labor market does not clear. This follows from basing the labor demand relation on traditional microeconomic theory of the firm and from modeling wage setting behavior in real terms, implying that all behavior functions are homogeneous of degree zero in absolute prices (and the quantity of money). The real variables, then, are in fact determined in a labor market subset of the model, just as in classical economics.

After the real variables have been determined in the labor market subset, the price level is determined to equilibrate demand and supply in the aggregate product market (equation 4.6a), with aggregate product demand assumed to be a negative function of the price level due to the real balance effect (M/P) and the influence of the real exchange rate ($e \cdot P^*/P$).

Although the (quasi)equilibrium solution of the model presupposes that product prices have adjusted fully, the model is nevertheless also a useful benchmark for analyses of situations in which the aggregate price level adjusts to shocks only gradually—that is, where nominal prices and wages are "sluggish."[7]

Figure 4.1 will serve as our basic workhorse in the subsequent discussion. The model could have been given alternative geometric representations, for instance, by a more conventional demand-supply diagram of the product market with the price level and output on the axes. (See appendix C for such a representation.)

The QERU concept, as already defined, is somewhat similar to but not identical with the natural rate and the NAIRU (nonaccelerating inflation rate of unemployment). The latter concepts are usually defined as requiring not only that the real wage rate is constant—that the rates of change in the nominal wage rate and price level coincide—but also that both rates of change are constant. By contrast, the QERU requires only these rates of change to be equal but not necessarily constant. Thus, denoting nominal values by capital letters, and the proportional rate of change by a caret: while the NAIRU requires that $\hat{W} = \hat{P}$ and that $\hat{W}$ and $\hat{P}$ are constant (if productivity growth is zero), the QERU, as defined up to now, requires only the first of these conditions: that $\hat{W} = \hat{P}$.[8]

A more definite modification of (or even break with) the notion of a natural rate and the NAIRU will be made later, when various mechanisms of unemployment persistence are introduced.

What would happen if the economy, for some reason, has wound up outside the QERU? Dynamic stability then requires the real wage to fall to the left of the QERU and rise to the right of it. In other words, the nominal wage rate has to increase less (fall more) than the nominal price to the left of N_o, and increase more (fall less) to the right of N_o. ($\hat{W} < \hat{P}$ when $N/\bar{N} < N_o/\bar{N}$, and $\hat{W} > \hat{P}$ when $N/\bar{N} > N_o/\bar{N}$.)

Suppose, for instance, that for some reason (to be elaborated below) the economy has wound up at point c in figure 4.1a, with the product wage rate w_1, aggregate employment N_1, and unemployment u_1. At this "high" level of unemployment, the wage setting ambitions, as expressed by the WS curve, are too weak to be consistent with the labor demand relations, as expressed by the LD curve; unemployment is too high for quasi-equilibrium in the labor market. In the context of union monopoly models, union bargaining models, and insider-outsider models, we can say that the wage setting ambitions of workers are too weak at this high level of unemployment for the prevailing product wage, w_1, to be sustainable. In the context of efficiency wage models, the product wage is unnecessarily high to keep down quitting and shirking and/or to maintain the quality of work applicants.

This assumed relation between deviations from the QERU, on one hand, and the rate of change in the real wage rate, w, on the other, is depicted in figure 4.1c. The assumption is consistent with traditional inflation-augmented Phillips curve analysis, according to which wage inflation rises with falling unemployment rates and a higher trend of price inflation and that price inflation rises with higher excess demand for products and a higher trend of wage inflation. (I leave open the question of whether the inflation variable in wage-Phillips curves should be interpreted as the currently observed inflation trend or expected inflation.) If such Phillips curve–type wage and price dynamics are formally added to the extended LD-WS model, it is easy to show that the quasi-equilibrium position b is a stable node, under the reasonable assumption that the cross-market effects on nominal wages and prices are weaker than the own-market effects (see appendix B).[9]

Such nominal wage and price dynamics of the Phillips curve–type build on empirical generalizations rather than traditional microeconomic theory. The microeconomic foundations for all types of price and wage dynamics, including Phillips curve dynamics, are quite weak.[10] Macroeconomics cannot, however, afford to abstain from exploiting whatever commonsense and empirical generalizations are available—and generalizations about nominal wage and price dynamics are available. We should not deny what we see only because we do not understand it—or because existing microeconomic theories cannot explain it.

In spite of much scorn of wage and price Phillips curves during the last four decades, there is strong empirical support for the conventional macroeconomic wisdom of the 1960s concerning wage and price dynamics (Tobin 1972), which was exploited in the stability discussion. Indeed, I will subsequently provide some rationale for such traditional aggregate price and wage dynamics.

Although the extended LD-WS model turns out to have many advantages, at least two long-term predictions of the model must, on the basis of the empirical evidence discussed in chapter 1, be regarded as artifacts. First, a rise in the size of the work force would, according to the model, generate a trendwise rise in the unemployment rate. This is easy to see. According to equation 4.1, a shift in $\overline{N}$ that is followed by a proportional shift in N leaves w unchanged. Hence, at the wage rate w_0, the WS curve shifts horizontally in the same proportions as $\overline{N}$. It follows that the new intersection point along the LD curve implies a smaller rise in quasi-equilibrium employment than in the labor force.

Second, the model does not rule out that gradually rising labor productivity generates a long-term trendwise change in the unemployment rate: there is no guarantee that rising labor productivity in the long run shifts the WS curve upward by the same amount as the LD curve, which would be required to avoid a (negative) long-term trend in the unemployment rate. These are certainly weaknesses of the model, since in the real world we hardly notice any long-term trend in the unemployment rate.

The model can be modified, however, so as to remove both of these dubious long-run properties. For instance, Layard, Nickell, and Jackman (1991, p. 107) show that the long-term (equilibrium) unemployment rate, in the context of a union monopoly model, is independent of labor productivity if the retention ratio of the unemployment benefit system (B/wN) is constant. In the context of insider-outsider models in which labor market flows and wage bargaining are explicitly modeled, the long-term unemployment rate is independent of both labor productivity and the size of the labor force, provided the retention ratio is constant, the wage rate is proportional to the firms' fallback revenue, and there is also free entry of firms (cf. Lindbeck and Snower 1991c). In both types of models, a key reason is that under these conditions, the wage setting curve becomes vertical in the long run.

As an illustration, it is easily seen from figure 4.1a and the underlying equations that if the WS curve happens to be vertical, the unemployment rate is independent not only of labor productivity but also of the size of the labor force. (For any level of w, a vertical WS curve shifts in proportion to the labor force, $\overline{N}$, according to equation 4.1.)

In the subsequent discussion, I assume these long-term properties of the wage setting curve to hold.

• • •

It may be of interest to pinpoint some similarities and differences between the analytical structure just presented and both
standard Keynesian analysis and the new classical macroeconomics. Along with the old and new classical macroeconomics,
the model presented here is characterized by a dichotomization
between a real sector, which determines the real variables, and
a nominal sector, which determines the price level. This property follows from having behavior functions that include only
relative prices and real variables—functions that are homogeneous of degree zero in absolute prices. Thus, as in old and new
classical macroeconomics, proximate determination of the level
of aggregate employment occurs, in the long run, in the labor
market. This is the case in our analysis despite the fact that the
employment level is determined by the equality between a
labor demand relation and a (real) wage setting function, rather
than between labor demand and labor supply, and that involuntary unemployment exists in our basic model.

The main similarity between traditional Keynesian models and
our model is that the labor market does not necessarily clear, in
contrast to classical models. A basic difference is that the nonclearing labor market in our analysis has explicit microfoundations. Moreover, whereas aggregate output and employment in
Keynesian-type models are determined by the equality of sav-
ing and investment, hence in an aggregate product market in
these models, here they are determined in the labor market, just
as in classical models. The latter difference tends to disappear,
however, in the context of short-term analysis of the effects of
product demand shocks, if sluggish prices and/or wages are

introduced into the analysis, as will be done later in this book. Thus, in conformity with "new Keynesians," the subsequent analysis respects the empirical fact that nominal prices and wages do not jump after various types of disturbances—that is, they are sluggish—which then implies short- and medium-term nonneutralities of monetary and exchange rate changes and other nominal disturbances.

5   Supply Shocks

Identifying a shock means specifying which of the changing variables in a model should be regarded as exogenous in the analysis. It is a matter of where the analysis should start.

The subsequent discussion of supply and demand shocks will be pursued in the context of figure 5.1 (which is an application of figure 4.1). For convenience, the four basic behavior functions in the preceding chapter are reproduced—the wage setting function (WS), the labor demand relation (LD), the product supply function (PS), and the product demand function (PD)—as well as equilibrium conditions in the labor and product markets. The first three equations determine w and N, and the last three determine P, after w and N have been determined:

$$w = G(\underset{(+)}{N/\overline{N}}, \underset{(+)}{b}, \underset{(+)}{B}) \qquad \text{(WS function)} \qquad (4.1)$$

$$w_d = D(\underset{(-)}{N}, \underset{(+)}{b}, \underset{(-)}{m}) \qquad \text{(LD function)} \qquad (4.2a)$$

$$w = w_d \qquad\qquad\qquad\qquad\qquad\qquad\qquad\qquad (4.3)$$

$$Q = Q(N, b) = J(\underset{(-)}{w}, \underset{(+)}{b}, \underset{(-)}{m}) \qquad \text{(PS function)} \qquad (4.4)$$

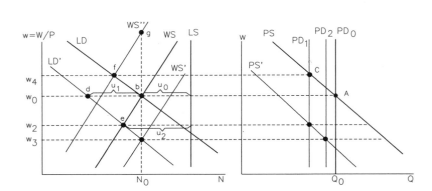

Figure 5.1
Effects of supply shocks

$$Q_D = K(M/P, e \cdot P^*/P, Q, A). \qquad \text{(PD function)} \qquad (4.5)$$
$${\scriptstyle(+)} \quad {\scriptstyle(+)} \quad {\scriptstyle(+)} \, {\scriptstyle(+)}$$

$$Q_D = Q \qquad\qquad\qquad\qquad\qquad\qquad\qquad (4.6)$$

We start with supply shocks, postponing the issue of demand shocks to the next chapter.

Technology Shocks

Theoretically, perhaps the most obvious example of a supply shock is an exogenous technology shock, which in this model is represented by a change in the productivity parameter b. However, while it is a commonplace to regard a considerable fraction of long-term aggregate productivity growth as a result of changes in applied technology, it is much less reasonable to interpret short-term fluctuations in measured aggregate productivity as the result of positive and negative technology shocks. We would instead expect the law of large numbers to make sudden short-term changes in the technology of individual firms even out for large aggregates, hence creating a rather smooth technology trend. Moreover, doubts that empirically observed short-term fluctuations in aggregate output can realistically be seen as the result of technology shocks are strengthened by numerous empirical studies of the diffusion of technology, which indicate that new techniques spread among firms and products only gradually and rather slowly.

For completeness, however, and as a preparation for the subsequent discussion of more realistic cases, let us start by looking at the consequences of assumed exogenous short-term shifts in aggregate (marginal and average) productivity—that is, shifts in the parameter b in equations 4.1, 4.2a, and 4.4. Neglecting, to begin, the direct impact on the wage setting curve, a negative technology shock may be depicted as a downward shift of the labor demand relation, for instance, from LD to LD' in figure 5.1a, and a corresponding leftward shift of the product supply curve from PS to PS' in figure 5.1b.

Let us also assume that, initially, the product wage does not change at all (denoted in figure 5.1a as a horizontal wage setting curve in the very short term). As a result, aggregate employment temporarily moves to point d, and unemployment increases by u_1. There are several reasons why the product wage rate may not adjust initially after a productivity shock. It may take time, in particular perhaps for workers, to realize that a productivity shock has occurred. Moreover, wage contracts last for certain periods of time, and they may be indexed. A third reason is that workers (and their unions) may insist that firms should bear the consequences of negative productivity shocks, especially perhaps if workers believe that the shock is temporary. A fourth reason is that workers (and their unions) may have developed norms of fair real wages, which may depend on previous wages; it might take some time to adjust these norms (in particular, perhaps, downward).

If the product wage instead adjusts freely to the new quasi-equilibrium position along the WS curve, the economy would wind up at the new quasi-equilibrium position e, with the product wage rate w_2 and unemployment u_2. For equilibrium in the product market, the product demand curve (equation 4.5) then has to shift from PD_0 to PD_1 either by way of restrictive demand management policy (lower M, e, or A), or by a rise in the price level sufficient to induce the necessary leftward shift of the PD curve. (In a diagram where the product market is depicted in (P, Q) space rather than (w, Q) space, there are movements along the product demand function; see the representation of the model in (P, Q) space in figure C.1 in appendix C.)

This schematic discussion is only a first step in a comprehensive analysis. In particular, as the productivity parameter (b) also enters the wage setting function, the downward shift of the labor demand relation is accompanied by a downward shift of the wage setting curve as well. Unfortunately, the various theories of wage setting behavior discussed so far do not have sufficient structure to make predictions about the size of the shifts of the wage setting curve relative to the shift of the labor demand relation (except possibly in the very long run). In order to bring about a return to the initial employment level, however, the wage setting curve would have to shift down exactly as much (vertically) as the labor demand relation—to WS'— with the quasi-equilibrium product wage w_3.[1] The PD curve would then not have to shift so much to the left as in the previous case to equilibrate the product market (it only has to shift to PD_2).

Granting the empirical observation that the unemployment rate in the long run is independent of labor productivity, we may hypothesize that in the long run, the wage setting curve tends to shift as much as the labor demand relation; these shifts will then generate a vertical long-run wage setting curve (at employment level N_0, with given labor force).

Price Increases for Imported Inputs

A sudden rise in prices of imported intermediary products is certainly a more realistic example of an exogenous negative shift of the labor demand relation in an individual country, although, in a worldwide perspective, such price shocks may often be realistically interpreted as endogenous responses on the world economy level to other economic events. Such price increases may be treated analytically (approximately) as negative productivity shocks for an individual country: real value added falls for given inputs of capital and labor (Bruno and Sachs 1985). Moving outside the formal model presented so far, the short-term dynamics may, however, differ considerably between the case of a negative proper exogenous technology shock and increased prices of imported intermediate inputs. In particular, we may hypothesize that the latter type of event results in an early (though gradual) rise in the aggregate price level, while a negative pure technology shock is perhaps less likely to have immediate effects of this type. One reason is that all firms in the former case would be expected to know that competing firms have been hit by a similar rise in input prices, while it is less obvious that an individual firm that experiences a sudden negative technology shock always expects other firms to have been hit by similar shocks.

This discussion of the effects of technology shocks and increased prices of intermediate inputs has been confined to a once-and-for-all shift in the aggregate labor demand relation and a corresponding shift in the product supply curve and wage setting curves. A more realistic case may be a slowdown in the rate at which both the labor demand relation and the wage setting curve drift upward. For instance, let us assume that both the labor demand relation and the wage setting curve have been drifting rightward at the same speed for some time but that the rightward drift of the labor demand relation suddenly slows because of an unexpected retardation of productivity growth or higher prices of intermediate inputs. Assume, however, that the upward drift of the wage setting curve continues as before because wage setters have not noticed the productivity slowdown or because they believe it to be temporary. As a result, aggregate employment would fall and unemployment would rise. Several economists have argued that such developments were important factors behind the rise in aggregate unemployment in the mid- and late 1970s (Bruno and Sachs 1985; Grubb, Jackman, and Layard 1982).

Partly in view of this experience, it is often argued that the varying ability of the product wage to adjust downward in response to negative productivity shocks, or rather to increased prices of intermediate inputs, is a crucial explanation of differences in unemployment experience among countries during the past two decades. For instance, it is often asserted that the economies in the United States, Japan, Austria, and Switzerland were quite successful in bringing down the product wage, without devaluations, after the oil price hikes and the slowdown in productivity growth in the 1970s.[2] In the context of the basic model in this book, it may be tempting to interpret this experience in terms of either a rather steep wage setting curve or a large downward shift of that curve (or both).

A similar interpretation is often made of the employment experience in Sweden, Norway, and Finland, where the product wage was also reduced considerably after the oil price shocks in the last half of the 1970s. This is a conventional explanation of why the rise in unemployment was relatively modest in these countries after the cost shocks in the mid- and late 1970s. It should be noted, however, that the apparent sensitivity of the product wage to changes in the unemployment rate in these countries was exhibited in the context of recurring discretionary devaluations rather than spontaneous market-induced product wage reductions by way of nominal wage moderation. It is open to doubt whether the fall in the product wage in these countries in connection with rather modest increases in unemployment can really be interpreted as high spontaneous sensitivity of the product wage to the unemployment rate. In other words, it is not obvious that an equally strong effect of higher unemployment on the product wage would have arisen without devaluations in these countries—an illustration of the Lucas critique, according to which estimates of structural equations are contingent on assumed behavior patterns of the government. More generally, the example illustrates the dangers of using econometric methods without looking at the mechanisms that have actually generated the data.

What has to be explained, then, is why nominal wages in the devaluing countries did not increase immediately (or at least within, say, a year) in proportion to the devaluations. In other words, where did the short- and medium-term nonneutralities of exchange rate changes come from? One obvious explanation may be that the devaluations in these specific cases were unexpected and that nominal wage contracts last for one or two years. This could not be the whole story, however, because the reduction in the product wage was maintained for many years (in some cases, for more than half a decade). Another explanation may be that it normally takes time for a devaluation to penetrate the entire input-output system of intermediary products—an issue to be taken up in the next chapter in connection with the effects of product demand shocks. A third (complementary) explanation may be that there was general agreement in these countries among the government, firms, employees, and unions that the product wage was too high to be consistent with desired levels of employment and perhaps also a desired rate of capital accumulation. As Keynes had already argued in the 1930s, employees and their unions may be willing to accept a real wage reduction in such a situation if they are convinced that all employees suffer real wage losses, which is exactly what a devaluation may achieve (at least for a while).

Increased Unemployment Benefits

Higher unemployment benefits (B) also shift the wage setting curve upward, which raises the product wage and reduces aggregate employment.[3] (The product demand effects of higher unemployment benefits are, again, left out for simplicity. But it is easy to combine the analysis of higher taxes later in this chapter with higher unemployment benefits, discussed here.) Unlike cost shocks through higher taxes or higher prices of intermediate inputs, which (for reasons given above) would be expected to raise the product wage only temporarily, higher unemployment benefits would be expected to exert a permanent effect on the wage setting curve by permanently raising the alternative income that is available for workers. We would then also expect a permanent increase in the quasi-equilibrium unemployment rate. The price level would rise.[4]

It is rather generally agreed that aspects of the unemployment benefit system other than the level of benefits also have important consequences for the unemployment level. Examples are the length of the period during which unemployment benefits can be received, the strictness with which they are administrated, and social acceptance of living on the dole among citizens in general. Indeed, Layard, Nickell, and Jackman (1991b, ch. 3.) assert, on the basis of their empirical studies, that country differences in the duration of unemployment benefits is the most important explanation of cross-country differences in unemployment rates (the second most important factor is asserted to be the degree of coordination among employers in wage bargaining).

Public works programs and tax-financed retraining programs for unemployed workers would also be expected to shift the wage setting curve upward, for the same reasons as higher unemployment benefits do. Indeed, studies for Sweden provide even stronger support for the predicted effects of such actions on wage setting behavior than for higher unemployment benefits. The reason might be that workers regard participation in public works programs as a closer substitute for ordinary work than living off unemployment benefits and perhaps also that workers and unions expect the government to expand such programs if unemployment goes up (that is, if private agents expect accommodating labor market policies).

Several studies for Sweden indeed suggest that if workers who lose their jobs are mopped up by public works programs, real wages will not fall much, if at all (Calmfors and Forslund 1990; Calmfors and Nymoen 1990; and Holmlund 1990). Thus, at least in Sweden, there is strong evidence of crowding-out effects of increased public works and retraining programs on private employment, as compared to higher open unemployment. This is a potentially important point, as policy recommendations of Keynesian economists have emphasized rather strongly the possibilities that public works programs expand output and employment in the private sector by way of multiplier effects. It is conceivable, however, that the Swedish experience is more relevant for small, highly open economies with fixed exchange rates and with comparatively low unemployment rates than for large and more closed economies with floating exchange rates and higher unemployment.

Nominal Wage Hikes

Another important issue concerns the effects of exogenous nominal wage hikes. Ideally, nominal wage changes should be treated as endogenous rather than as exogenous events. After all, an important task of macroeconomic analysis is to explain nominal wage changes as a result of changes in other economic variables, such as the labor market situation, the inflation trend (or expected inflation), productivity growth, and the profitability of firms. However, some nominal wage hikes in the real world have turned out to be difficult to explain by using traditional explanatory variables. Obvious examples include the notorious European wage explosion around 1970 and in some European countries again around 1975. Various authors have tried to endogenize these events by interpreting them as the result of, for instance, stronger bargaining powers of unions in connection with new labor market legislation, increased union militancy—that is, changes in union preferences (Layard,

Nickell, and Jackman 1991b)—or possibly a delayed effect
of previous profit increases over 1965–1970 (Lindbeck 1980).
Occasionally, however, we may have no other realistic alternative except to treat an observed nominal wage hike as just an
exogenous event.

The question remains, however, as to why firms are unable to
prevent a nominal wage increase from resulting in a rise in the
product wage, and hence in an upward shift of the WS curve,
by way of increasing product prices in proportion to the nominal wage hikes. There are at least four reasonable explanations
for this.

First, in countries with large-scale price indexation of wages,
workers receive automatic compensation for price increases after sudden exogenous nominal wage hikes, which means that
the initial increase in the product wage may prevail for a considerable period of time—at least until a new round of collective bargaining occurs.

Second, if monetary and fiscal policies are nonaccommodating,
firms may be unable to shift higher nominal wages fully onto
output prices, which means that the product wage would go up.

Third, international competition in the product market may imply that the product prices of domestic firms are rather strongly
tied to world market prices. Domestic prices would then (in the
case of a fixed exchange rate) be influenced not just by domestic wage costs and domestic aggregate product demand parameters but also by the foreign price in domestic currency ($P^* \cdot e$).
With fixed exchange rates, the product price would then be
expected to rise less than the nominal wage would in response

to nominal wage hikes, with a rise in the product wage, W/P, as a result.

Finally, in an open economy with a fixed exchange rate, employment may fall even if domestic product prices increase in proportion to higher nominal wages, so that the real wage, as defined by $w = W/P$, is unaffected. The reason is that the price of domestic output in this case would tend to rise relative to the price of foreign output; in other words, the real exchange rate $P/(P^* \cdot e)$ would rise, so that "our" country would partly be pricing itself out of the world market. Indeed, this was the reason for including the real exchange rate in the product demand function in chapter 4. (There are numerous examples of this from the real world.) As a result, a nominal wage hike will exert a negative effect on aggregate world demand for domestic aggregate output, assuming a fixed (or only partly accommodating) exchange rate. How this may influence aggregate employment and unemployment is one of the issues analyzed in the next chapter.

In order to characterize the mechanism already discussed, it is useful to introduce a different concept of the real product wage than that used earlier: the product wage expressed in international rather than domestic prices, that is, $W/(e \cdot P^*)$ rather than W/P. The former certainly increases by higher W even if firms would shift higher nominal wages fully onto higher prices of domestically produced goods (P). This concept of the real product wage corresponds to the real exchange rate expressed in domestic wage units.

Most of the supply shocks discussed here have one feature in common: they tend to raise the product wage rate (w) relative to labor productivity (b), at least temporarily. The difference between these two variables, the so-called wage gap ($w - b$), became a popular analytical device during the 1970s and 1980s in much of the applied macroeconomic literature dealing with various types of supply shocks. Indeed, according to various empirical studies, the "wage gaps" in Western Europe as a whole tended to increase by some ten percentage points in the mid-1970s (see, for instance, Bruno and Sachs 1985; various issues of OECD *Economic Outlook* in the early 1980s; Artus 1984). It has turned out to be difficult, however, to explain country differences in unemployment experiences by wage gaps (Gordon 1990), partly perhaps because of measurement problems and partly because of the influence of other variables on the outcome.

Indeed a basic problem with attempted empirical quantifications of wage gaps is the difficulty of separating exogenous shocks from endogenous responses. For instance, observed changes in labor productivity may be either a cause or an effect of changes in the product wage. More specifically, let us assume an upward shift of the wage setting curve from WS to WS" in figure 5.1a. We would then like to measure the wage gap as an ex ante concept, by the vertical distance between the new wage setting curve and the old labor demand curve at the initial employment level N_o; the ex ante wage gap would be the distance bg. The reason for using an ex ante wage gap concept is that we want to regard the opening up of the gap as a cause of the subsequent change in the level of employment. In reality, however, wage gaps have usually been measured at the actual employment level, which has been influenced by the original shift of the wage setting curve. For instance, suppose that after the nominal wage shock, the economy adjusts to point f at the intersection of the LD and the WS" curves; here the wage gap has been eliminated ex post. A tendency to eliminate the ex ante wage gap in this way is one basic reason that existing empirical estimates of wage gaps do not provide reliable measurements of the magnitude of the initial shocks, although interesting attempts have been made to calculate ex ante wage gaps (Artus 1984). But such difficulties in empirically quantifying the magnitude of wage gaps should not lead us to dismiss the usefulness of the concept of an ex ante wage gap as a theoretical construct. Moreover, even wage gaps that are calculated ex post may provide some information about ex ante wage gaps because of the time lags before such gaps are closed.

Higher Tax Rates

Higher tax rates may also influence aggregate employment and unemployment in this framework. In order to examine this issue, it is necessary to make a distinction between the real consumption wage and the (real) product wage. Let us define the real consumption wage:

$$w_c = W(1 - t_i)/[P_c(1 + t_c)],$$

where P_c is the consumer price index and t_i and t_c are the income and consumption tax rates, respectively. Denoting the payroll tax rate by t_w, the product wage may then be written,

$$w_p = W(1 + t_w)/P = w(1 + t_w).$$

By dividing the expression for w_c by the expression for w_p we get

$$w_p = w_c \cdot \theta \cdot \lambda, \tag{4.7}$$

where $\theta = [(1 + t_w)(1 + t_c)]/(1 - t_i)$ and $\lambda = P_c/P$. We call θ the tax wedge and λ the price wedge. It is also useful to define P_c as a function of the domestic product price and the price of foreign goods, $P_c = \gamma(P, e \cdot P^*)$, and to assume that this index function is homogeneous of degree one in P and $P^* \cdot e$.

Let us now assume that the wage setting process, as defined by equation 4.1, refers to the real consumption wage rather than the production wage. This is the most reasonable interpretation of the wage formation process in all the various microtheories of wage setting that were discussed in chapter 3. Thus, equation 4.1 may be rewritten as

$$w_c = w_p/\theta\lambda = G(N/\overline{N}, b, B),$$

or

$$w_p = w(1 + t_w) = \theta\lambda \cdot G(N/\overline{N}, b, B). \qquad \text{(WS function)} \qquad (4.1')$$

The labor demand relation now reads

$$w(1 + t_w) = D(N, b, m). \qquad \text{(LD function)} \qquad (4.2a')$$

The equilibrium condition is

$$\theta\lambda \cdot G(N/\overline{N}, b, B) = D(N, b, m) = w(1 + t_w). \qquad (4.3')$$

In terms of figure 5.1, the model may now be interpreted as having $w(1 + t_w)$, rather than w, on the vertical axis. A rise in t_w, t_c, or t_i now shifts the WS function vertically; for every value of N, a higher w_p is required in the wage setting process.

Let us now assume an exogenous rise in the payroll tax rate, t_w, so that θ increase. To any desired consumption wage (w_c) there now corresponds a higher product wage (w_p) than before (see equation 4.7). In terms of figure 5.1a, with $w(1 + t_w)$ rather than w on the vertical axis, the quasi-equilibrium point would move from point b to point f, with the new product wage w_4 and lower aggregate employment. In terms of figure 5.1b, equilibrium in the product market then requires the product demand curve to move to the left, through higher product prices, so that it intersects the PS curve at point C.[5]

The magnitude of the negative employment effects of such a wage-tax increase depends not only on the size of the shock but also on the elasticities of the labor demand and wage setting curves—and hence on the extent of the shift of the payroll tax increase onto prices and wages, respectively. Econometric studies suggest that these effects differ among countries. Several studies for Sweden, for instance, indicate approximately fifty-fifty forward shifting onto prices and backward onto wages, respectively, in the perspective of a few years (Holmlund 1983). In the long run, however, it is tempting to hypothesize a rise in the payroll tax to be borne, in real terms, mainly by wage earners, assuming that the long-run rate of return on capital in an individual country cannot deviate much from that in the rest of the world. Moving outside the formal model, this development may, in the context of figure 5.1a, be depicted as a tendency of the wage setting curve to shift down again toward its initial position, by way of a gradual downward adjustment of the consumption wage, w_c, and hence also of the product wage, $w(1 + t_w)$.

Owing to such mechanisms, higher payroll taxes have often been asserted to be one of the factors behind the rise in unemployment in the 1970s in some European countries. But they cannot possibly have been responsible for the further rise in unemployment in the first half of the 1980s, since at that time payroll taxes were not increased to any large extent.

According to equation 4.7, income taxes and consumption taxes have, in principle, the same comparative statics effect on wage setting behavior as payroll tax increases. However, again moving outside the model, the short-term dynamic effects would be expected to be rather different. Higher income or consumption tax rates would, in the real world, initially be expected to reduce the after-tax consumption wage, w_c, rather than to raise the product wage of firms (as payroll taxes do immediately), since the nominal wage rate would not be expected to rise immediately. This heuristic reasoning may be represented in figure 5.1a, again with $w(1 + t_w)$, rather than w, on the vertical axis, by only a very modest upward shift (or no shift at all) of the wage setting curve in the very short run in response to higher t_c or t_i, in contrast to an immediate upward shift in the case of a higher payroll tax.[6]

To do full justice to the analysis of changes in tax rates, it would also be necessary to look at the consequences for product demand, which requires a specification of what the higher tax revenues are used for: increased government spending, less money creation, or reduced borrowing. My analysis, which is designed to highlight supply shocks, stops short of these considerations. The next chapter deals with such issues by discussing the consequences of variation in aggregate demand in the product market.

• • •

Obviously, different types of supply shocks have different implications for the correlation between changes in the product wage and employment. Exogenous productivity shocks and exogenous price changes for intermediate inputs would be predicted to result in procyclical movements in the product wage; these types of shocks, by shifting the labor demand relation, induce movements along an upward-sloping wage setting curve, assuming that this curve does not shift much as a result of the shock. Increased payroll taxes, higher unemployment benefits, and nominal wage hikes, by contrast, would be expected to result in countercyclical movements in the product wage rate; such shifts would generate movements along a downward-sloping labor demand curve by shifting the wage setting curve, assuming that the labor demand relation does not change much. The much stronger tendency toward countercyclical movements in the product wage in Western Europe than in the United States during the post–World War II period perhaps depends on recurrent upward shifts of the wage setting curve in Western Europe—probably due to fluctuations in the aggressiveness of often rather strong unions, payroll tax increases, and changes in unemployment benefit systems throughout the 1970s.

Thus, it is not possible to discriminate between supply shocks and demand shocks merely by looking at the correlation between changes in product wages and unemployment; the sign of the correlation between the product wage and employment in the case of supply shocks depends on the type of supply shock under study. The issue is blurred by the fact that it is not clear how changes in product wages and employment are correlated in the case of demand shocks either. In general, a reason for this is that the relative flexibility of nominal wages and nominal prices, in response to product demand shocks, may differ both over time and among countries.

6   Demand Shocks

Although Keynesian macroeconomics originally emphasized product demand shocks, the methodological difficulties in analyzing them are still pronounced. This is the case not only in models in which the labor market clears, such as in (new and old) classical macroeconomic theory, but also in models with real wage rigidity and excess supply of labor, provided the structural equations are homogeneous of degree zero in absolute prices (and nominal money balances). The basic reason is that in all such models, aggregate employment is determined in the labor market; this also applies to the LD-WS model presented in chapter 4.

When discussing this issue, it is useful to distinguish three classes of transmission mechanisms, each expressed in terms of characteristics of the labor demand relation (in product wage and employment space): (1) movements along a given, downward-sloping labor demand relation, (2) movements along a horizontal or possibly even upward-sloping labor demand relation, and (3) shifts of a downward-sloping labor demand relation. Our discussion of these three possibilities is based on the LD-WS model (chapter 4) with a nonclearing labor market—that is, a product wage that is rigid in the sense that it does not adjust to the point of intersection of the labor demand relation (the LD curve) and labor supply (the LS curve). Only when classical and new classical theories are referred to—as a comparison to the LD-WS model—will it be assumed that the product wage is fully flexible in the sense that the labor market clears. As the subsequent analysis identifies and compares different types of transmission mechanisms, it is unavoidable that we also enter fairly well-known territory.

Movements along a Downward-Sloping Labor Demand Relation

Let us depict the representative firm of our model in price-output space (figure 6.1) by way of a conventional microeconomic diagram. Assuming that the product demand curve

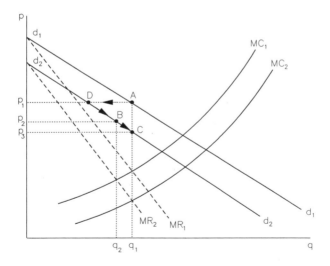

Figure 6.1
Output determination under monopolistic competition

is originally $d_1 d_1$ and the marginal cost curve MC_1, the profit maximization point is A, with the price level p_1 and the output level q_1. A drop in the product demand curve to $d_2 d_2$—for instance, due to a fall in M—then changes the profit maximum point to B, with lower product price and output in the most likely case—assuming, for the time being, that the nominal product price is fully flexible while the nominal wage rate, and hence also the MC curve, is unchanged.

The same story may be told in figure 5.1, with an initial shift of the aggregate product demand curve, say from PD_0 to PD_1 (at unchanged nominal wages). With flexible prices but, to begin with, fixed nominal wages, there is a movement up along the downward-sloping product supply function (in product wage and output space) and a corresponding movement up along the downward-sloping labor demand relation, and hence a fall in aggregate employment. For instance, there may be a move from point A to point C in figure 5.1b, and from b to f in figure 5.1a. This is simply the transmission mechanism of product demand shocks in Keynes's *General Theory* and several generations of Keynesian textbooks—"Keynes I" for short—as well as in models with sticky and staggered nominal wages (in the manner of Stanley Fisher, Jo Anna Gray, and John Taylor).

But this is only the beginning of the story. Assuming (as before) that all behavior functions are homogeneous of degree zero in absolute prices and money balances and that the nominal wage is flexible in the long run, the nominal wage rate will ultimately fall until the marginal cost curve is MC_2, so that the system returns to the initial output level (q_1), although now at a lower price level (p_3) than the initial one. In the context of figure 5.1b, prices and wages will fall until the PD curve has moved back to the initial position at PD_0, but with lower nominal prices and wages than initially; in figure 5.1a, the economy returns to point b. These are, then, the consequences of aggregate demand shocks in a world where product prices are fully flexible while nominal wages adjust only slowly.

This cannot, however, be a general theory of the transmission of product demand shocks to the labor market. There is no a priori reason that prices should always (systematically) respond to product demand shocks faster and more strongly than wages. In terms of figure 6.1, a downward adjustment of the nominal wage rate, and hence a downward drift of the MC curve, may very well occur before product prices start to fall. The initial adjustment to lower aggregate output and employment may therefore take place with a constant, or falling, rather than a rising product wage rate. Indeed, the product wage rate in the real world does not systematically seem to move countercyclically in response to product demand shocks (which Keynes himself also admitted a few years after publication of *The General Theory*).

There are, however, empirical examples of countercyclical movement of the product wage rate. One case in point is the simultaneous rise in the aggregate product wage rate and fall in aggregate employment in several developed countries in the 1930s (although in the United States it was the real consumption wage more than the real product wage that increased); similar developments took place in Western Europe in the 1970s. By contrast, it is a commonplace that there is no consistent countercyclical pattern for the product wage in the United States after World War II. This is probably one of the main reasons that Keynesian macrotheorists in the United States have recently more or less abandoned the Keynes I model, instead turning to models that allow acyclical or even procyclical movements of the product wage. As a consequence, they have emphasized rigidity of nominal prices rather than nominal wages.

The rather different behavior of the product wage in the United States and Western Europe after World War II is somewhat of a paradox. On a priori grounds, we may hypothesize that nominal wages would be more sensitive than product prices to domestic product demand shocks in Western Europe, which would then tend to create a procyclical product wage rate (in response to products demand shocks) in that part of the world. The reason is that while the labor market is approximately a nontradable sector, the product markets in West European countries are quite open to international competition, which should make product prices rather closely tied to world markets, while wages would be expected to react more briskly to changes in the domestic economy. In the less open U.S. economy, we may expect nominal prices to be more closely influenced by domestic demand shocks than in Europe, with a better chance for a countercyclical pattern for the product wage. From this point of view, it is surprising that the empirical evidence instead points in the opposite direction: there have probably been stronger tendencies for the product wage rate to move countercyclically in Western Europe than in the United States.

The paradox is accentuated by the observation that wages in the United States are frequently determined in nominal terms for several years ahead (often three years), while wage contracts in Europe are usually shorter and often include price index clauses. These factors would also be expected to contribute to a better chance for a countercyclical pattern for the product wage in the United States than in Western Europe. There is no obvious explanation for this paradox. One possibility is that

Western Europe has been more exposed than the United States to supply shocks in the form of nominal wage explosions and related product wage increases (in terms of figure 5.1, upward shifts of the wage setting curve), with reduced aggregate employment as a result.

Moreover, employment-stimulating reductions in the product wage in the tradable sector have occasionally occurred in some countries in Western Europe due to discretionary devaluations and related reductions in the product wage; this, again, generates movements along the labor demand relation. Exchange rate policies may have considerable real effects for long periods of time, even though they would be expected to be ultimately unsuccessful due to the homogeneity (of degree zero) of the behavior function. Suppose, for instance, that a sudden devaluation of the exchange rate, when starting from a quasi-equilibrium position, has reduced the product wage and raised aggregate employment; that is, it generated a movement down the LD curve in figure 5.1a. In the real world, it might take quite a long time, perhaps several years, for the product wage rate, and hence the macroeconomy, to return to the initial equilibrium (at point b in the figure). A real-world illustration is the reduction in the product wage in Sweden and the ensuing fall in unemployment from about 3.5 percent to about 1.5 percent in connection with the devaluations in 1981 and 1982. It seems to have taken more than half a decade for wages and prices to adjust fully to the devaluation. Similar examples can be given for many other countries, such as Norway and Finland during the 1970s and 1980s. This illustrates the possibility of pursuing exchange rate policies for the purpose of exploiting temporary nonneutralities for several years, although we may speculate that sooner or later, recurrent devaluations will shorten the adjustment period over time.

Similarly, a devaluation may be used as a method of speeding up the return to quasi-equilibrium if the economy happens to be outside that position. Post—World War II experiences of such defensive devaluations are plentiful. This type of devaluation is perhaps the most appropriate use of exchange rate policies for employment purposes, although at the cost of higher inflation than the outside world—and the risk of expectations of future devaluation and continuing, or perhaps even increasing, inflation.

This discussion has assumed a nonclearing labor market; an alternative interpretation of fluctuations in aggregate employment is that they are instead generated by fluctuations in the point of intersection of an aggregate demand and supply curve for labor in a clearing labor market. An example is Milton Friedman's worker-misperception model, according to which employee households misinterpret wage and price inflation, generated by expansionary monetary policy or a devaluation, as a rise in the real consumption wage. The effect is a rightward shift of the labor supply function (in product wage and employment space) and an ensuing fall in the actual real product wage and a rise in aggregate employment. However, the Friedman hypothesis could easily be turned on its head by hypothesizing that workers instead (mistakenly) believe that wage and price inflation reduces real wages. (Complaints to this effect among employees are quite common during periods of inflation, even if nominal wages in fact rise at least as much as prices.)

The worker-misperception model is hardly strengthened if it is combined with the Lucas-Rapping hypothesis that higher (perceived) wages today relative to wages tomorrow, or higher interest rates today, result in intertemporal substitution of leisure today for leisure tomorrow. As has often been pointed out by critics of that hypothesis, the elasticity of the intertemporal substitution of leisure seems to be too small in the real world to make this an empirically important theory.

The Lucas supply curve, based on misperceptions among firms rather than among workers—the "imperfect information model"—encounters similar problems. The "firm," which in this version is simply a self-employed worker, is mistakenly assumed to interpret unexpected inflation as a rise in the real price (in terms of consumer goods) of its output good and accordingly increases its supply. This model is basically just a more sophisticated version of Friedman's model, with a more explicit analysis, in a stochastic context, as to how the misinterpretation of the market signals is supposed to occur; that is, it includes a signal extraction analysis. It is difficult, however, to regard such a hypothesis of misconception as a general theory since it builds on quite arbitrary assumptions about systematically biased misunderstandings of firms, in spite of the availability of information on aggregate prices in the mass media. In other words, while the general idea of rational expectations—that is, that private agents use all available information—is reasonable, the assumed information set is not. It is somewhat surprising that economists who strongly emphasize the rationality of private agents in collecting and interpreting information have to rely so heavily on systematic (biased) information mistakes ("misunderstandings") to be able to explain observed short-term macroeconomic fluctuations.

While Friedman's worker misperception model, Lucas-Rapping's intertemporal leisure-substitution model, and Lucas's imperfect-information model all assume that wages equilibrate supply and demand for labor, this assumption is not a necessary property of theories built on misperceptions. Such phenomena may also be incorporated in models with a nonclearing labor market. Assuming, for instance, that wage setters (such as unions) underestimate the price increase after a positive product demand shock, they may accept nominal wage contracts that turn out to result in real wage reductions (for given levels of employment). As a result, the WS curve in figure 6.1 would shift (down) to the right, with a movement down the LD curve, and a lower actual product wage and higher employment as a result, just as in Friedman's and Lucas's models.

Movements along a Horizontal or Upward-Sloping Labor Demand Relation

Another possibility of avoiding the tyranny of the downward-sloping labor demand curve is to argue that this curve is not always downward sloping in the relevant segment. For instance, during the first phase of a business upswing, firms often have underutilized capital assets—idle machines and empty assembly lines. The individual firm may temporarily be able to expand labor inputs and capital services (from capital goods installed earlier) simultaneously even in the short run. Employment may then increase without a fall in the marginal product of labor; the latter may even increase if labor and capital services are sufficiently strong complements (Lindbeck and Snower 1988b). This kind of mechanism operates, of course, only if there is excess capacity of the capital stock within firms. Maybe this is the situation that is implied in macro models in which there is assumed to be constant returns to labor (as an example, see Blanchard and Summers 1987).

A horizontal or an upward-sloping segment of the labor demand relation, however, is not sufficient to explain why a positive product demand shock may result in increased employment without an accompanying fall in the (real) product wage rate. It is also necessary to explain how movements may arise along the (horizontal or upward-sloping) labor demand relation— why, that is, the wage setting curve (in the context of figure 5.1a) would tend to shift down (to the right) in response to positive product demand shocks. It is possible, however, to identify some plausible mechanisms for such real effects. For instance, because prices of imported goods are components of the consumer price index, an unchanged real consumption wage does not require nominal wages to rise in proportion to an increase in the prices of domestically produced goods. This means that the product wage may fall, for given levels of employment, without an accompanying reduction in the real consumption wage. (This possibility has been emphasized by Calmfors 1989.) The wage setting curve (in product wage and employment space) would fall as a result. However, the generality and quantitative importance of such effects are open questions.

Shifts of the Labor Demand Relation

How, then, can changes in aggregate demand in the product market result in shifts of the labor demand relation, in (w, N) space, rather than induce movements along it? When examining this issue, it is useful to distinguish between shifts when product prices are flexible and shifts that require price stickiness.

Flexible Prices

Keynesian-inspired macroeconomics often imply that shifts of the aggregate product demand curve induce shifts of the labor demand relation—also without explicitly assuming sticky prices. This procedure is reflected in the habit (as in Layard and Nickell 1986; Solow 1986) of writing the aggregate labor demand relation with not only the real wage rate but also an aggregate product demand parameter as arguments—in our notation, $N_d = F(w, b, A)$, where A reflects the level of aggregate demand in the product market.

The basic weakness of this specification is that microeconomic labor demand relations, in the context of a clearing product market, reflect parameters of the production function (and, in the case of imperfect competition, also the elasticity of the product demand curve) but not parameters that define the level of product demand. The reason is that the conventional labor demand function of an individual firm simply reads $n_d = f'^{-1}(w/(1 - m))$, where $f(n)$ is the production function, and m is Lerner's measure of monopoly power, where $m = 1/\eta_F = \mu/(\eta \cdot s)$, with η_F denoting the elasticity of product demand of the individual firms, η the price elasticity of aggregate product demand, s the number of firms, and μ the conjecture coefficient expressing the expected change in aggregate output by an individual firm when it changes its own output by one unit (see Lindbeck and Snower 1986b and appendix A). (A small value of μ means that aggregate output is assumed by the individual firm to increase very little when it expands its own output, which may be interpreted as a rather atomistic market structure.) Of course, $1/(1 - m)$ is the traditional markup of prices on marginal labor costs, which follows from the marginal condition for profit maximization—

$$p = W/f'(n)(1/(1 - m)).$$

In the simplistic case of identical firms, the aggregate labor demand relation may then be written as

$$N_d = s \cdot f'^{-1}(w/(1 - m)), \tag{4.2b}$$

which is a more explicit formulation of the previously assumed LD curve—equation 4.2. Accordingly, a product demand shock shifts the aggregate labor demand relation in (w, N) space only if at least one of the variables η, μ, $f'(\ )$, or s changes. How likely are such changes in response to product demand shocks?

A vast literature argues that the aggregate product demand elasticity (η) rises by higher product demand, so that m falls and the aggregate labor demand relation shifts to the right (Pigou 1927; Kalecki 1938; Keynes 1939; Stiglitz 1984; Rotemberg and Saloner 1986). In other words, the markup of price over marginal (labor) costs is assumed to fall by higher product demand. In terms of the notations above, it is assumed that the variable m in equation 4.2a is a stable positive monotone function of A, so that the labor demand function (equation 4.2) may, in fact, be written $N_d = F(w, b, A)$ rather than $N_d = F(w, b, m)$.

It is quite likely that changes in the elasticity of product demand and/or the conjecture coefficient, and hence the monopoly power of the individual firm, do change by variations in aggregate demand in the product market and hence shift the aggregate labor demand relation. There is also a possibility that product demand shocks will change the composition of product demand with respect to products or households with different price elasticities, so that the price elasticity of aggregate product demand will change (this possibility is discussed in Lindbeck and Snower 1988b). However, the assumption of a systematic, and sufficiently strong, positive relation between aggregate product demand, on one hand, and η and/or μ, on the other hand, seems to be a rather weak peg on which to hang a general theory of the transmission of product demand shocks to aggregate output and employment.

Systematic transmission mechanisms via $f'(n)$ constitute another possibility by which aggregate product demand shocks may raise aggregate output and employment. For instance, increases in some specific types of government expenditures, in particular infrastructure investment, may increase labor productivity in private firms, and hence shift the labor demand relation to the right. The tyranny of the negatively sloping labor demand curve is in this case overcome by a shift of that curve. However, this cannot possibly be an important short-term mechanism, as the construction of infrastructures takes considerable time (often longer than the business cycle). If we look at the development of output and employment in a somewhat longer time perspective, such as a decade, increased spending on public sector infrastructure may very well be an important factor behind shifts of the labor demand relation. Perhaps the strong development of output and employment in the private sector in the OECD countries during the 1950s and 1960s was to some extent related to the heavy investment in infrastructure that took place during these decades.

Entry of new firms, and hence an increase in s, is another conceivable transmission mechanism of aggregate product demand shocks to the aggregate labor market. Although not modeled in this book, the general idea of this mechanism is that increased product demand raises profit, which in turn induces the entry of new firms. (We may hypothesize that a temporary fall in the product wage is part of this mechanism; see Lindbeck and Snower 1988b.) The potential importance of the entry of firms for higher employment is highlighted further by the insider-outsider theory, because in new firms there are no insiders who may exploit a business upswing to push up their own wages rather than allow increased hiring. Unfortunately, there has not been much research on the quantitative importance of the entry of firms for the expansion of aggregate employment in various countries.

It may be tempting to argue that the difficulty of establishing transmission mechanisms from product demand to the labor market is an artifact of the assumption that there is only one factor of production in the model: labor. More specifically, intuition may suggest that when a positive product demand shock increases the demand for capital goods and intermediate inputs of firms, the increased inputs of these factors will raise the marginal product of labor and, accordingly, shift the labor demand relation to the right, provided these inputs are technological complements to labor. (Indeed, this is sometimes argued in the literature; an example is Solow 1986.)

This is a misleading way of looking at the issue however. Capital goods and intermediate products do not fall down into the production process like manna from heaven; these inputs are determined simultaneously with labor inputs. Consequently, while the earlier labor demand relation was written $N_d = C(W/P, b, m)$, in a model with an intermediate input and a capital good, the relation may be rewritten $N_d = C^*(W/P, P_i/P, P_k/P, b, m)$, where P_i and P_k denote the prices of the intermediate input and the capital good, respectively. This means that the previous analysis of the consequences of product demand shocks is not changed in principle. More specifically, an analysis of the transmission mechanism of product demand shocks to the labor market must indicate how the shocks affect the relation between labor demand and the real wage after endogenous variations in the demand for all inputs have been

taken into account. In other words, the labor demand relation
that is relevant for an analysis of the transmission mechanism
is not the conditional one (the relation between labor demand
and the real wage when all other inputs are held constant) but
rather the unconditional one (allowing other variable inputs
to change).

It is easy to show that the slope of the labor demand relation is
greater (the LD curve is flatter) when labor and intermediate
products are interdependent, in the sense that these inputs
are either complements or substitutes (Lindbeck and Snower
1988b). The intuitive reason is that when they are complements, a rise in labor demand is associated with a rise in the
demand for the intermediate good, which in turn raises the
marginal product of labor. When labor and the intermediate
input are substitutes, a rise in labor demand is associated with a
fall in the demand for the intermediate input, which again raises
the marginal product of labor (since labor and the intermediate
good in this case are substitutes). Consequently, the change in
the marginal product of labor (and thus the slope of the labor
demand relation) must be greater than it would be in the absence of factor substitutability; indeed, whenever the degree of
factor interdependence is sufficiently large, the labor demand
relation will be horizontal or even upward sloping. (This is
simply a generalization of the earlier discussion of the possibility that the labor demand function may be horizontal, or even
upward sloping, when capital is not fully utilized in the firm
after a product demand shock.)

Thus, a product demand shock does not result in a shift of the
labor demand function (for given values of η, μ, $f'(\ )$ and s) even
though the relative price of the intermediate product changes in
connection with the change that the firm chooses to make in its

output price (P). This change in the relative price of the inter-mediate input is already reflected in the slope of the LD curve.

Of course, an exogenous shift in the price of the intermediate input itself (in P_i) has supply-side effects on labor demand, as discussed in chapter 4. For instance, a rise in P_i shifts the labor demand relation down to the left. Thus, to the extent that an expansionary domestic product demand shock increases the price of the intermediate input (P_i), labor demand will be nega-tively affected if the intermediate product is a complement to labor. In other words, the introduction of intermediate inputs into the production function does not help to explain transmis-sion mechansims of product demand shocks. In the case of imported intermediate inputs, a change in the exchange rate will exert a similar supply-side effect. In a regime with a floating exchange rate where a rise in the quantity of money depreciates the exchange rate, $P^* \cdot e$ will rise and play the same role, in principle, as a negative supply shock on the demand for labor. This supply-side effect would counteract whatever positive ef-fects may emerge from increased M on labor demand via other channels. Hence, by introducing intermediate products into the model, we make it more difficult, rather than easier, to explain how expansionary product demand shocks may result in a rise in employment.

To summarize, I have identified three types of transmission mechanisms from aggregate product demand to aggregate out-put and employment in models where nominal prices and wages are flexible and the aggregate product market clears, in addition to the often asserted, but far from obvious, mechanism according to which positive product demand shocks generate systematic reductions in the markup of prices over costs (by way of changes in the elasticity of product demand of individual firms):

1. Infrastructure investment that raises the marginal product of labor and hence shifts the labor demand relation in individual firms to the right.

2. The entry of firms, which shifts the aggregate labor demand relation to the right.

3. Increased utilization of the capital stock within firms, which may result in a horizontal (or even upward-sloping) segment of the labor demand relation in the short run after a recession. In this case, shifts in the wage setting curve may generate changes in aggregate output and employment without a countercyclical movement in the product wage rate.[1]

Short-Term Price Stickiness

Most analytical attempts after World War II to explain why variations in aggregate product demand may shift the aggregate labor demand relation have not relied on mechanisms of the types outlined above but rather on short-term stickiness of nominal product prices. Indeed, such stickiness seemed to be the cornerstone of so-called new Keynesian macroeconomics during the 1980s.

The inspiration for analytical work along these lines probably comes from the empirical observation that firms in the real world, in a short- and medium-term perspective, often seem to respond to product demand shocks mainly by increased output, and often also employment, rather than by price increases, as long as the prices of inputs, including labor, have not increased. The aggregate product price level does not usually jump in response to aggregate product demand shocks; prices usually rise gradually.

In terms of figure 6.1, the new Keynesian macroeconomics hypothesis is that a negative product demand shock moves the price-output position from point A to point D at the predetermined price, p_1. (In terms of figure 5.1, the aggregate labor demand relation shifts to the left, say from LD to LD', with a fall in aggregate employment from point b to point d.) There is no reason to characterize this as a "disequilibrium" situation or a situation of nonclearing in the product market. The individual firm itself is assumed to choose ("voluntarily") to stick to the predetermined price, p_1, and to satisfy all demand at this price. There is no rationing of buyers or sellers. Thus, contrary to what is often asserted, models with imperfect competition in the product market do not really provide microfoundations for Barro-Grossman type "disequilibrium" models; individual firms voluntarily choose to keep product prices unchanged after a product demand shock.[2]

The new profit maximum point (B in figure 6.1), at flexible product prices and unchanged factor prices, would be approached only gradually, and when nominal wages have also fallen, the firm may adjust fully to the new macroeconomic equilibrium point C in figure 6.1. Thus, the asserted price-output trajectory may look, schematically, like the arrowed path in the figure.

The most difficult question concerning sluggish prices has not yet been asked: How do we explain asserted nominal price stickiness? (By "stickiness," I mean sluggish rather than fixed prices.) The most popular explanation in the 1950s and 1960s was to assume that prices are set by some rule of thumb, such as on the basis of fixed markups—for instance, on long-term marginal or average costs. There is not necessarily anything wrong with building theoretical analyses on such empirical generalizations of price setting behavior. It should be admitted, however, that until we have found a plausible microeconomic story behind observed behavior, we have not given a very profound explanation for observed phenomena.

One early attempt to construct a microeconomic theory of nominal price stickiness was to assume that the firm does not have good enough information about the marginal cost and marginal revenue functions to shift immediately to the new optimum (profit-maximizing) price-output combination (hence to point B or point C in figure 6.1). As a result, the firm was asserted to change output rather than the price in order to obtain better information on these matters; this attempted explanation can be traced back to Kalecki (1938). It is far from clear, however, why a firm would choose to change only output (and employment) rather than both price and output when it lacks good information about the marginal cost and marginal revenue functions. Rather, could it not be argued that the firm would get even better information about the demand curve by experimenting with price increases and reading off the ensuing effects on product demand?

The Greenwald-Stiglitz (1989) variation on this theme may be more promising; their argument is that there is greater uncertainty about the consequences for the firm's profits of a change in price than of a change in output. The reason would be that the firm has more information on conditions within the firm (such as marginal costs) than on conditions outside the firm (such as the consequences of price changes for sales). The importance of these uncertainty considerations is still an open question.

A second attempt has been to assert that the product demand curve of the individual firm is more elastic above than below the initial position. The classical theory of the kinked product demand curve as formulated by Sweezy is an example: firms are asserted to expect competitors to follow price reductions but not price increases. This theory has been exposed to much justified criticism over the years. There may be more to the new version of the kinked demand curve, relying on asymmetric information, according to which only old customers notice price changes (Stiglitz 1984; Woglom 1982). But how realistic, and important, is this assumption in a world of aggressive advertising about prices?

A third attempt has been to argue that the firm, for goodwill or long-term profitability reasons, does not change the price except in response to a cost increase (Okun 1982). This, then, would be an attempt to explain fixed markups. Although the idea appears to ring true, this approach has yet to be given a good microeconomic formulation. Some doubt may also be motivated on the grounds that the important aspect for a rational customer should be how high a price a specific firm charges relative to other suppliers rather than how high the price is relative to the production costs of the firm.

Perhaps it could also be argued that the realism of asserted fixed markups on costs is less convincing today than, say, in the early 1970s. We have recently seen considerable variability in markups (and profit margins) over time, in particular in the tradable sector. The internationalization of national economies, and the related increase in competition, may have reduced the

tendency of firms to adhere to rigid cost-plus pricing because of
high elasticity of product demand for individual firms on world
markets.

The most frequently discussed attempt recently to explain sluggish prices has no doubt been the menu cost theory. Its punch-
line is that small costs of adjusting prices may prevent the firm
from changing its price if the firm is originally at its profit
maximum point (where the profit function is flat) but that this
type of behavior may nevertheless have substantial macroeconomic effects (because output is socially suboptimal, to begin
with, when there is not perfect competition). However, the
logic of the theory may be questioned. If it is true that firms
often do not adjust prices to changes in product demand, then
firms would usually be off the profit maximum point when
shocks occur. And then it would not be true that the lack of
price adjustment after a product demand shock is connected
with only small (second-order) losses to the firm.[3]

The weak points of this theory from an empirical point of view
are rather well known (see, e.g., Lindbeck 1988; Blanchard and
Fisher 1989). It does not seem plausible that firms' costs of
changing prices (even with a liberal interpretation of the concept of costs) would be larger than the various adjustment costs
of changing output and, in particular, employment in response
to product demand shocks. Indeed, I have already argued that
the costs of hiring and firing labor are substantial. If this point
is correct, the menu cost argument may even be turned on its
head: firms would react to demand shocks by keeping output
and employment unchanged and letting prices adjust accordingly (to the extent that changes in inventories and delivery
lags would not bear the full adjustment).

It is also well known from various empirical studies that firms often change their prices by quite small amounts, which casts further doubt on the menu cost argument. Frequently it has been pointed out that in an inflationary world, prices are, in fact, often changed once or even several times a year. If aggregate demand suddenly expands, then the next time a firm changes its price, why would it not make the price change larger than it would have been otherwise?

For these reasons it is not obvious that we should emphasize various microeconomic costs or uncertainties in connection with price changes when trying to explain price stickiness and related quantity adjustments. An alternative and, in my view, more realistic explanation of sluggish product prices is to refer to delays in the transmission of price changes of intermediate goods between individual firms. Along such lines, Gordon (1990) has suggested that it is difficult for firms to predict future price changes of intermediate inputs, and hence to calculate the new rational expectation price vector after an aggregate product demand shock. Gordon therefore argues that a firm simply assumes prices of intermediate inputs to be unchanged until the firm itself is actually confronted with a price change for its purchases of intermediate inputs. This means assuming that firms systematically underestimate actually occurring changes in the price of intermediate products after increases in aggregate product demand. This assumed underestimation delays the ultimate effect of aggregate product demand shocks on the aggregate price level.

I agree with Gordon about the importance of delays in passing on price changes of intermediary products through the complex input-output system; however, it remains to be explained why the difficulties in predicting future price increases due to a product demand shock would necessarily result in a downward bias (rather than just random mistakes) of expected price changes for intermediate inputs.[4]

One approach may be to assume that there are production lags between intermediate inputs and outputs of individual firms, in a model in which outputs of individual firms are used as inputs in other firms. Since the marginal cost curve for many firms is often rather flat immediately after a recession (and the elasticity of product demand may be approximately constant), such a firm initially may keep the output price approximately unchanged and adjust its output after a product demand shock. Wages and some prices—for instance, of raw materials—may, however, start to rise quite soon after a positive product demand shock, and as a consequence the marginal (and average) cost curves would gradually shift upward also for firms with constant marginal costs in the relevant interval. Cost and price increases would then wander slowly through the input-output system.

Such a production lag model was recently formalized in Lindbeck and Snower (1991b). Formally, the firm decides its inputs in period $t - 1$, and these inputs are actually inserted into the production process in that period, although the output does not turn up until period t. The inputs inserted into the production process in period $t - 1$ cannot be sold separately afterward, such as in period t, because they have already been "contaminated." Thus, it is the market price of intermediate inputs in period $t - 1$, when the inputs are inserted into the production process, that matters for the price and output of the finished good in period t, and not the price that may emerge in the market after the production process has started (when the opportunity cost of the inserted "contaminated" intermediate product is zero).

In this specific model, firms are characterized by short-term sluggishness of their output prices in the sense that they set prices for a short period of time before demand shocks are observed. The production lags accentuate the consequences for macroeconomic price formation of this short-term price sluggishness in individual firms. In short, transient price precommitments can turn into prolonged price inertia as it works its way through the input-output system. Such price inertia, in turn, implies that the initial change in final demand has significant quantity effects. Production lags may be said to have a similar effect on aggregate price behavior in this model as staggered contracts in the price-staggering model of Blanchard (1983).

By using models with production lags in the context of complex input-output systems, we do not have to rely so much on asserted costs or uncertainties regarding price changes in individual firms. We can adhere to the traditional assumption that firms choose an optimum combination of price and output, as in the ordinary theory of imperfect (monopolistic) competition, although possibly with a short time lag before individual firms adjust prices to product demand shocks and changes in marginal costs. Sluggishness of product prices after product demand shocks is, then, quite consistent with profit maximization behavior and a clearing product market, without much reliance on microeconomic costs of price changes in the analysis.

• • •

There are, then, numerous potentially important transmission mechanisms of product demand shocks to aggregate output and employment, in models with flexible wages and prices and in models with nominal wage or price stickiness. But these mechanisms are much more complex, and in some cases also much less understood, than envisioned by early Keynesians.

It is important to note the different roles of real and nominal stickiness of prices and wages. Chapter 3 on alternative explanations for the existence of unemployment was concerned with real wage rate rigidity. This is not the type of rigidity that is relevant when we try to explain the effects of changes in aggregate product demand on aggregate output, employment, and unemployment. In this case, the crucial aspect is rigidity in nominal wages and/or prices: movements along the labor demand relation require sluggish nominal wages, and shifts of that relation may be generated by sticky nominal prices. Moreover, in the case of a change in the money stock, it is sluggishness in nominal prices that ensures that real money balances go up, thereby allowing domestic aggregate demand to increase.

7   Mechanisms of Unemployment Persistence

The apparent persistence of unemployment remains to be explained. This phenomenon may intuitively be understood either as slow, dynamic adjustment of the economy toward its (quasi-)equilibrium level of unemployment or as an endogenous change in the (quasi-)equilibrium unemployment rate itself under the influence of the previous path of unemployment. In both cases, unemployment is seen as time dependent, or path dependent. In empirical analysis, it is difficult, perhaps even impossible, to distinguish between these alternative interpretations of persistence. In reality, unemployment persistence is probably caused by several different mechanisms, so it is useful to take a brief look at different theories that propose to explain it.

One suggested mechanism of unemployment persistence is *capital shortage* (Malinvaud 1984; Sneessens and Drèze 1986). More specifically, slow accumulation of real capital assets during recessions is asserted to result in a capital stock that is too small to allow a swift return to the previous level of employment. In the context of figure 4.1a, a shift of the labor demand relation from LD to LD' would not be followed after the recession by a return of the labor demand relation to its initial position because of decumulation of the capital stock during the recession. As empirical support for this hypothesis, reference has been made to the combination of high unemployment and high levels of capacity utilization of the capital stock in some European countries during the second half of the 1980s. This theory implies that it is important to use models that include not only labor but also physical capital in the production function when analyzing unemployment.

The theory is incomplete, however, in the sense that a sufficiently large reduction in the product wage, or in the context of our model a sufficiently large downward (rightward) shift of the wage setting curve, would return aggregate unemployment to the prerecession level. In this sense, the argument that capital shortage may generate unemployment persistence implicitly assumes resistance to product wage reductions. Without such resistance to real (product) wage reductions, unemployment persistence would be prevented by, for instance, factor substitutions through increased shift work and the reallocation of resources to labor-intensive sectors. Another objection to the capital shortage hypothesis is that new investment may solve the problem within a few years. New machinery may be installed quite quickly; new industrial buildings can frequently be constructed within less than a year.

As pointed out by, for instance, Blanchard and Summers (1986), empirical evidence from the United States around 1940 also casts some doubt on the importance of the capital shortage explanation of unemployment persistence. Unemployment fell drastically at that time in connection with the sharp increase in aggregate product demand, largely due to rearmament, in spite of many years of low real investment. Another example is the brisk expansion of employment, and the huge reduction in unemployment, in the United States after the deep recessions in the mid-1970s and early 1980s, again after periods of rather low rates of capital formation. The fast reduction in unemployment in the United Kingdom in the period 1985–1990, also after a period of rather low capital formation, is a third example. Nevertheless, it is quite possible that the capital shortage explanation of unemployment persistence, in combination with downward sluggishness of product wage rates, has some explanatory power in a fairly short-term perspective.

A variation on the theme of capital shortage is that plants and firms may be permanently closed during prolonged recessions and that the entry costs of new plants and firms prolong the return to the prerecession employment level. Similarly, brisk entry of firms in a business upswing may have persistently positive effects on aggregate employment in the next downswing because the entry costs have already been paid (Lindbeck and Snower 1988b).

Unemployment persistence due to an asserted loss of human skills during prolonged recessions, and subsequent *human capital shortages*, would also be depicted in figure 4.1a as a labor demand relation, which, after a recession, is stuck (for a while) at a position like LD' rather than returning to the initial prerecession position, LD. It is often argued that such persistence-generating effects of long-term unemployment may be accentuated if employers use long unemployment spells as a screening device (that is, a signal of low-quality labor) (Meager and Metcalf 1987; Winter-Ebner 1991). A sufficient reduction in the product wage, and related factor substitution, however, could in principle mitigate the unemployment consequences of human capital shortage. Thus, this variant of the capital shortage hypothesis also has to be combined with an assumption of downward product wage rigidity. Moreover, it is not clear that skills are lost fast enough to make the hypothesis plausible in the first place.

The discouraged worker mechanism—the hypothesis that workers reduce their search activities during long unemployment spells —would instead, in the context of figure 4.1a, be depicted as an upward shift of the wage setting curve, as unemployed workers are assumed to exert less downward pressure on wages when job search diminishes. There are many variations on this theme in the literature. One is that during the course of their unemployment spells, workers gradually stop searching for jobs, at least after some time, because of a reduction in their subjectively assessed probability of finding a job match. This may very well be true, but the argument needs some modification. It is true that a fall in the subjectively assessed probability of a job match reduces the return to job search and, hence, creates a substitution effect away from job search. But this effect is counteracted by the fact that the worker has to search harder to get a job when there is less probability that given search activities will result in a job match, and this creates a positive (income) effect on search activities, which mitigates the former effect.

Perhaps the most celebrated variation on the theme of discouraged workers is that unemployed workers gradually acquire higher preferences for leisure or lose self-confidence during long periods of unemployment (see, for instance, Layard and Nickell 1986; Daniel 1990). However, this asserted effect, implying endogenous changes in preferences, has to be compared with the traditional search theory hypothesis that workers (with given preferences) gradually tend to scale down their reservation wage during the course of unemployment spells when they learn that their previous wage expectations were overly optimistic.

The discouraged worker effect is consistent with empirical data from the United Kingdom according to which long-term unemployed workers are characterized by relatively low probabilities of leaving the unemployment pool. There is also evidence from Phillips curve studies that long-term unemployed workers exert less downward pressure than do short-term unemployed on both the product wage level and the rate of nominal wage increase (Layard and Nickell 1986). One problem in interpreting these results is that it has turned out to be difficult to distinguish between the discouraged worker hypothesis and a selection process by which long-term unemployed workers largely comprise those who are intrinsically less productive than others.

There are also some empirical data that conflict with the hypothesis that the long-term unemployed search less than the short-term unemployed. Using detailed panel data from the United Kingdom, Blanchflower and Oswald (1990) conclude that the estimated effects of the length of unemployment spells on the product wage level disappear if the relation between unemployment and wage formation is assumed to be nonlinear. Moreover, in Sweden, the probability that an individual will leave the unemployment pool does not seem to fall by the length of the individual's unemployment spell (Björklund 1990). Because the level of aggregate unemployment was very low in Sweden during the period under study, perhaps the Swedish experience suggests that discouraged worker effects arise only if unemployment has become a common and socially acceptable form of life, and, hence, an unemployment culture has been created. Thus, the discouraged worker effect seems plausible enough to be taken quite seriously.

Labor turnover costs provide another possible explanation of unemployment persistence. It is well known that such costs, at given wage rates, have ambiguous effects on the average level of employment over the business cycle, as both hiring and firing would be predicted to fall. What is clear, however, is that labor turnover costs create employment inertia at the historically given employment level and generate persistence in the sense of high serial correlation of both aggregate employment and unemployment (Bentolila and Bertola 1990; Lindbeck and Snower 1988, ch. 9, 10). In terms of figure 4.1a, the labor demand relation would shift to the right only reluctantly in connection with changes in factors that, in the absence of labor turnover costs, would generate increased labor demand.

The social implications of labor turnover costs depend, however, on the type of macroeconomic instability that happens to exist. Figure 7.1a is a schematic illustration of the role of labor turnover costs in the case of ordinary business cycles, on the basis of the previous discussion. The solid curve represents the predicted employment path in a country with high labor turnover costs and the broken curve the aggregate employment path in a country with low labor turnover costs. It does not make economic sense for a firm with high labor turnover costs to fire, and later rehire, employees if it expects to need them again soon. Here is one conceivable explanation as to why the employment path was smoother in Western Europe (with relatively high labor turnover costs) than in the United States in the period of ordinary business cycles during the first three decades after World War II.

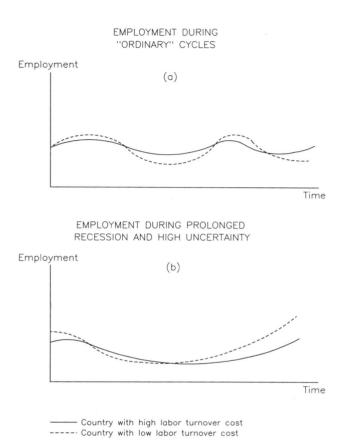

Figure 7.1
Cycles and employment

The situation is quite different after a long and deep recession; not only countries with low but also those with high labor turnover costs may have experienced a substantial reduction in aggregate employment. Firms in countries with high labor turnover costs would be expected to be particularly reluctant to hire labor in a subsequent business upswing if there is considerable uncertainty among firms about the sustainability of the ensuing upswing, because firms are then highly uncertain about whether they really need more labor in the near future. This point is illustrated in figure 7.1b, where the solid curve represents a country with high turnover costs, such as a typical West European country, while the broken curve represents a country with low turnover costs, such as the United States. Perhaps this was the situation in the early 1980s. Firms in Western Europe were much more reluctant than firms in the United States to engage in new hiring after the prolonged recession, perhaps with considerable uncertainty about the sustainability of a new upswing in the early 1980s.

Thus, differences in labor turnover costs may help explain the stark differences in aggregate employment performance between the United States and Western Europe in both the early postwar period, with ordinary business cycles, and during the 1970s and 1980s, with prolonged recessions. This explanation, however, is only an untested hypothesis.

These points may be of particular importance for small firms. In the case of a large firm, it may not be so dangerous to wind up overstaffed. Natural attrition (quitting and retirement) often solves the problem of overstaffing, since large firms often have both high quitting rates and a wide distribution of employees in different age groups. The situation is more serious for small firms. Many of them often have relatively low quitting rates, and in contrast to large firms, some may not have any employees close to retirement age.

This discussion so far has been confined to the direct effects of labor turnover costs on employment persistence. Nothing has been said about the indirect effects via wage formation. This is where *the insider-outsider theory* of employment reenters; the wage setting behavior of insiders may accentuate the persistence effect of labor turnover costs. The insider-outsider theory also fills an important lacuna in the other explanations of unemployment persistence. For example, the capital shortage hypothesis and the screening hypothesis lack an explanation as to why reduced wage demands by outsiders cannot compensate for reduced (conceived) productivity of unemployed workers. The insider-outsider explanation of unemployment persistence is illustrated in figure 7.2, which is an elaboration of figure 3.1.

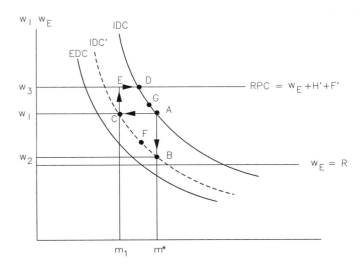

Figure 7.2
Unemployment persistence

Suppose that an unexpected negative productivity shock occurs or, more realistically, a sudden increase in the prices of imported intermediate inputs, when the initial number of insiders is m^*. The new insider demand curve is assumed to be IDC', as compared to the initial demand curve IDC. To simplify the exposition, but without any basic loss of generality, let us assume that the wage rate is initially at point A, with the wage rate w_1.

It is useful to discuss the consequences in the context of two extreme alternative responses of the wage rate. One extreme case occurs when insiders are anxious for all of them to keep their jobs, so that they are willing to accept a wage reduction to w_2; as a consequence, the wage-employment point would move from A to B. This outcome is particularly likely if there is no seniority system among workers, so that each incumbent worker is faced with the same risk of being fired if the wage rate is not reduced. A similar outcome may emerge if there is a special form of profit-sharing system, in the sense that the remuneration of workers is automatically tied to the marginal revenue product of workers.

At another extreme, insiders insist on keeping the earlier wage, w_1, and the firm agrees. Some workers are laid off, and the firm moves from point A to point C in figure 7.2. This outcome is particularly likely if there is a well-defined seniority system, so that a majority of workers are confident that they will not be fired even if the product wage is unchanged. The argument builds on the assumption that the majority of workers do not care much about the employment status of the workers who become fired.

Thus, in general, the employment consequences of a negative labor demand shock depend on the system of remuneration, the presence (or absence) of seniority, and the preferences of high-seniority workers regarding other workers.

The insider-outsider theory may explain not only the existence of unemployment but also the occurrence of layoffs. More specifically, the remaining high-seniority workers may prevent wage underbidding from laid-off workers by threatening not to cooperate with them, as well as by threatening to harass them if they try to keep their previous jobs by underbidding the initial wage rate.

For the purpose of the subsequent analysis, let us assume the second of these extreme cases—the wage rate does not adjust downward after a negative labor demand shock. Assume further that the insider labor demand relation later returns to the initial position (IDC in figure 7.2). If the insiders now care enough about the employment opportunities of the workers who were fired earlier, they may accept keeping the product wage at w_1 and allowing the firm to move back to point A, rather than exploiting the situation to raise their wage rates further. All previously fired workers (or substitutes for them) may then be rehired. This case would imply that while the insiders are egotistical enough to insist on an unchanged wage rate immediately after the initial negative shock, they are altruistic enough to accept that the workers who were fired earlier (or substitutes for them) get their jobs back when the labor demand curve returns to the initial position. This might be particularly likely if the period of bad times has been short, and the previously fired workers are still unemployed and living in the same community as the employed workers rather than having moved to other regions.

Another obvious possibility is that after the return of the labor demand curve to the initial position, insiders try to exploit the improved labor demand situation to push up their wages to the highest possible level without being fired—to the wage w_3 in figure 7.2. This means that the firm will choose point D, with only a modest increase in employment. In this case, a negative labor demand shock in one period also tends to keep down the employment level in the future, even after the temporary shock has been reversed. It should be kept in mind, however, that this model does not predict full hysteresis, in the sense that this term has been used recently in the labor market literature (Blanchard and Summers 1986).[1] The employment level does not stay at m_1 after the labor demand curve has shifted back to the initial position; rather, it winds up at a level (point D in the figure) between the initial level (m^*) and the level after the negative shock (m_1), if insiders are willing and able to exploit their market power fully.

There are many other possibilities. For instance, after the initial negative shock, insiders may opt for a combination of lower wages and lower employment, as indicated by point F in figure 7.2. Similarly, they may opt for a combination of higher wages and higher employment after the labor demand curve returns to the initial position, as exemplified by point G. Such behavior would be stimulated not only by insiders' genuine concern for the situation of (potential) outsiders but also by unions' ambitions to have many members (for exemple, to achieve financial and political strength).

This discussion does not mean that we would necessarily expect a succession of equally large negative and positive shocks to result in a trendwise reduction in employment. After the wage rate w_3 at point D has been reached, further shocks will have symmetric effects, because insiders cannot push up their wage above w_3 (at the RPC line) without being replaced by outsiders. Moreover, in the real world, we would expect positive productivity shocks to dominate negative ones, as reflected in the positive productivity trend over the medium and long term.

In reality, labor is a rather heterogeneous factor of production, often with technical complementarities between different types of labor. Moving outside the formal model, it is therefore often in the interest of remaining insiders that attrition (quitting and retirement) is followed by new hiring of workers to prevent a fall in the productivity of remaining workers.

If a negative labor demand shock in period t results in a fall in employment and insiders in period $t + 1$ exploit a later reversal of the shock to push up the wage rate, the latter becomes a negative function of the initial employment level: the lower the level of employment is in a given period, the higher the product wage rate would be in the next period. Such a negative relation between the employment level in one period and the wage rate in the following period, however, is not a general inference from the insider-outsider theory. For example, suppose that the negative shock had been somewhat smaller, or somewhat larger, than indicated by the shift of the labor demand relation from IDC to IDC'. The economy would wind up at point D after the reversal of the negative shock—at the same position as when the insider demand relation shifted to IDC'. Thus, the insider-outsider theory does not provide a general reason for assuming that the employment level in the preceding period has a negative influence on the wage setting equation. This underscores the point that it is not reasonable to test the insider-outsider theory by looking at the relation between the employment level in one period and the wage rate in the next period.

• • •

In general, it may be concluded that there are several plausible mechanisms of unemployment persistence. It is too early to say which of these mechanisms are the most important ones in the real world. Some of them not only complement each other but may also interact in complex ways. All of the theories discussed, except the capital shortage mechanism, emphasize labor market dynamics. While according to the discouraged worker explanation, unemployment persistence depends on the behavior of the long-term unemployed, in the insider-outsider model, it depends on the behavior of insiders, although their behavior is influenced by conditions in the open labor market. The insider-outsider theory also allows persistence to depend on the distribution of aggregate unemployment in short- and long-term unemployed workers. This requires, however, that insiders care less and less about outsiders the longer the latter have been unemployed. We may in this case say that the degree of outsidedness of unemployed workers increases as the length of unemployment spells increases.

It is often argued that unemployment persistence increases by the unemployment rate. Indeed, some theories of unemployment persistence suggest such a relation.[2] As pointed out in chapter 2, figure 2.1 does not, however, give a strong impression of such a relation. This is an aspect that should be subjected to more empirical studies.

If, as I have argued, unemployment persistence is largely the result of labor market dynamics, the construction of the unemployment benefit system is a potentially important factor behind unemployment persistence. Regarding the unemployment experience in Western Europe in the 1970s and 1980s, we may say that not only did the shift to a more liberal unemployment benefit system in the 1970s (Layard, Nickell, and Jackman 1991) contribute to a rise in the quasi-equilibrium unemployment rate, as discussed in chapter 4, but the continued existence of such a system may have accentuated unemployment persistence in the 1980s, although no further liberalization of the benefit system took place.

8   What Have We Learned?

Answers to the Questions

Three basic questions about the issue of unemployment were asked in chapter 1.

The first was why unemployment exists at all and how the levels of aggregate employment and unemployment are determined. An answer to the first part requires an explanation of why existing wages are not underbid by unemployed workers. While minimum wage regulation is probably the most obvious explanation, it was argued that such regulation is not a major reason for aggregate unemployment in developed countries. Social norms that make underbidding of prevailing wages a socially unacceptable form of behavior probably provide a more general explanation for nonmarket-clearing wages. But this explanation is quite shallow if we do not also explain how such norms emerge, in whose interest they exist, and how they are upheld. It was also argued that union models—either union monopoly models or, more realistically, union bargaining models—go a long way toward explaining nonmarket-clearing wages. Union models by themselves, however, do not explain why unorganized workers do not try to get jobs by underbidding existing wages and succeed in doing so. Thus, like social norms, union models require some microeconomic under-pinnings to qualify as deep explanations of nonmarket-clearing wages.

Various versions of the efficiency wage theory also provide important explanations of nonmarket-clearing wages, and hence of the existence of unemployment. The main limitation of this set of theories is perhaps that they attribute a very passive role to workers and unions in the wage setting process. While efficiency wage theories postulate that it is not in firms' interest to reduce nonmarket-clearing wages, various versions of the insider-outsider theory argue that it is not in the interest of incumbent workers to do so. Like other theories, this one should be amended to explain why more sophisticated types of contracts than time contracts do not emerge, such as contracts that would make it possible for outsiders to get jobs by sharing the potential gains from higher employment with incumbent workers (insiders).

All of these theories of nonmarket-clearing wages may be regarded as complementary rather than competing theories. For instance, efficiency wage mechanisms, insider-outsider mechanisms, and union bargaining may be combined in the same model. Moreover, some versions of the efficiency wage theory, in particular, George Akerlof's theory of gift exchange between firms and workers, do explain the existence of wage norms. And some versions of the insider-outsider theory help explain the market power of unions, the existence of social norms against wage underbidding, and the support for minimum wage legislation among a majority of workers.

In the context of a simple macroeconomic model with a clearing product market and a nonclearing labor market, aggregate employment and unemployment are determined by the intersection of a labor demand relation (the LD function) and a wage setting curve (the WS function). This approach, which has recently been developed and applied by several macroeconomists, helps explain fluctuations in aggregate employment (and unemployment) without requiring a high elasticity of substitution between leisure and income or between leisure in different periods.

The second question in the introduction was how supply and demand shocks may precipitate changes in the levels of aggregate employment and unemployment. While exogenous productivity shocks and exogenous price changes for imported intermediate inputs are predicted to result in procyclical movements in the product wage, increased payroll taxes, higher unemployment benefits, and nominal wage hikes would rather be expected to result in countercyclical movements. Thus, all types of supply shocks cannot be identified as causing countercyclical movements in the product wage.

The analysis of the employment consequences of product demand shocks encounters the same type of problems in macro models with a nonclearing labor market as an analysis in the context of classical and new classical models, as long as all behavior functions are homogeneous of degree zero in absolute prices. This book's analysis of transmission mechanisms of product demand shocks is built on a distinction of movements along a downward-sloping labor demand relation, movements along a horizontal or upward-sloping labor demand relation, and shifts of the labor demand relation. I argued that movements along a downward-sloping labor demand relation are more convincingly explained as a result of sluggish nominal wages than of misinterpretations of inflation as real or relative wage and price changes. Movements along a horizontal or even upward-sloping labor demand relation were discussed mainly in connection with variations in capacity utilization, which may make the marginal product curve horizontal or even upward sloping. The possibility that product demand shocks generate shifts in the labor demand relation was dealt with in the context of both flexible and sluggish product prices. In the case of flexible prices, four channels of transmission were identified: changes in the elasticity of aggregate product demand, changes in the conjecture coefficient that expresses how other firms are expected to react to a variation in output by an individual firm, changes in the marginal product of labor, and changes in the number of firms.

Efforts were also devoted to examining alternative microfoundations of nominal price sluggishness as an explanation for the transmission of product demand shocks to output and aggregate employment. Reference was made, in particular, to the gradual transmission of cost impulses among firms via the prices of intermediate products, with less emphasis placed on recently popular hypotheses regarding the role of costs and uncertainties of price changes in individual firms (such as so-called menu costs).

The third question I posed was how to explain the apparent persistence of unemployment, often even after reversal of the initial impulse that precipitated the change in unemployment. After reviewing several suggested explanations, I emphasized two hypotheses: the discouraged worker effect and explanations in terms of labor turnover costs and their consequences for wage formation.

Country Experiences

It is not my purpose in this short book either to set forth a comprehensive analysis of the unemployment experience in individual countries or to report attempted empirical quantifications and tests of alternative theories of unemployment, but I will add some real-world flesh to the theoretical bones by schematically reporting and interpreting the unemployment experience in three countries: the United States, the United Kingdom, and Sweden. (For comparison, a diagram of the inflation and unemployment experience of the EC as a whole is also included. Table 2.2 reports unemployment statistics in the OECD countries.)

The U.S. experience is interesting because of the drastic expansion of aggregate employment during the 1970s and 1980s and the relative volatility of aggregate employment and unemployment in that country. The experience in the United Kingdom illustrates an economy with pronounced tendencies toward unemployment persistence, although it was largely overcome during the second half of the 1980s. The Swedish experience is singled out because this country has generally been regarded as a success story in terms of employment policy, although the reasons for this success, in my judgment, have been largely misunderstood by both domestic and, in particular, foreign observers.

The unemployment and inflation experiences in the United States and the United Kingdom from 1960 are illustrated in figures 8.1 and 8.2. When inflation was at a (local) peak level around 1980, the U.S. and the U.K. authorities introduced highly restrictive economic policies, mainly monetary policy, apparently to squeeze inflation out of the system. Probably as

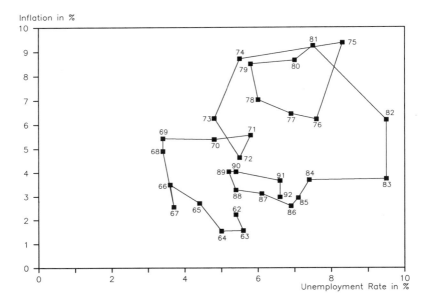

Figure 8.1
Price-Phillips curve for the United States, 1962–1992. Source: OECD, *Economic Outlook*, no. 50 1991. Note: Inflation is defined as the percentage change in GDP deflator.

a consequence of such policies, the traditional Phillips loops in both countries were transformed into superloops between 1980 and 1990, as depicted in the figures.

The subsequent expansionary fiscal policy in the United States is probably a main reason for the rapid fall in unemployment, in particular after 1983. In figure 8.1, these monetary and fiscal policy experiences show up as the "Volcker-Reagan loop" between 1980 and 1988. The most likely explanation for why the fall in unemployment started later in the United Kingdom than in the United States is that fiscal expansion also started later.

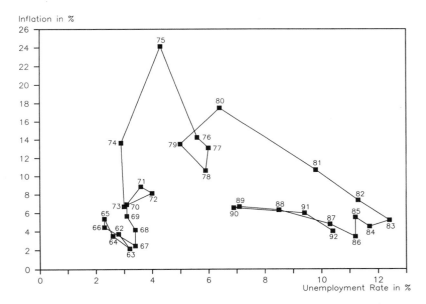

Figure 8.2
Price-Phillips curve for the United Kingdom, 1962–1992. Source: OECD, *Economic Outlook*, no. 50 1991. Note: Inflation is defined as the percentage change in GDP deflator.

Many observers were worried that inflation increased somewhat during the period of falling unemployment, in spite of the fact that unemployment was still rather high by historical standards. One possible explanation is the rather high speed at which unemployment fell, particularly in the United Kingdom, during the period 1986 to 1989, an explanation that is in conformity with the hypothesis that not only the level but also the rate of change in unemployment influence the rate of wage increase. This is consistent with persistence theories predicting that both the current and the previous levels of (un)employment, and hence also changes in unemployment, influence the rate of nominal wage increase.

An important stylized fact that needs to be explained is the strong trendwise increase in aggregate employment in the United States, relative to most other countries, during the 1970s and the first half of the 1980s. The most apparent explanation is perhaps that the United States experienced a rather labor-intensive type of output expansion, and hence a very weak increase in labor productivity. In a sense, the United States, bought rapid employment growth by way of very slow growth in labor productivity. In the context of traditional microeconomic theory, such development was made possible by rather stagnant product wages (as illustrated in table 2.2, columns 3–5), which created incentives to labor-intensive production. From this point of view, wage formation in the United States responded in a quite rational way to the fast growth in the labor force. The other side of the coin was unavoidable: a slow rate of increase in labor productivity.

This is probably not the only reason for the slow rate of labor productivity growth in the United States. Total factor productivity growth—growth in production per unit of input of labor plus capital—was also considerably slower in the United States than in Western Europe (Abramovitz 1991). Attempts to find explanations for this have recently become a growth industry in itself among economists in the United States; this issue, however, is outside the scope of this book.

The Phillips loops in the EC as a whole look rather similar to the loops in the United Kingdom (figure 8.3). Basically, figure 8.3 probably reflects the consequences of the highly restrictive, anti-inflationary economic policy in most EC countries during

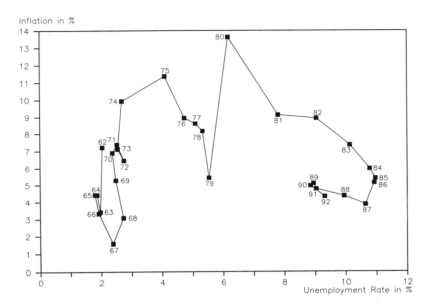

Figure 8.3
Phillips curve for the EC, 1962–1992. Source: OECD, *Economic Outlook*, no.
50 1991. Note: Inflation is defined as the percentage change in GDP deflator.

the period 1980–1985 and the only moderately expansionary
policy stance after 1985.

It may be interesting to contrast the United States, the United
Kingdom, and the general EC experiences with the experience
of a small, open economy. International interest in Swedish
unemployment performance may make it useful to choose that
country as an example. Indeed, it is often asserted in the international literature that Sweden has solved the unemployment
problem and that other countries would be well advised to
follow the Swedish example. Swedish unemployment and infla-

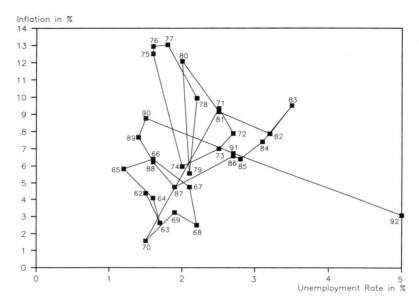

Figure 8.4
Price-Phillips curve for Sweden, 1962–1992. Source: OECD, *Economic Outlook*, no. 50 1991. Note: Inflation is defined as the percentage change in GDP deflator.

tion experiences are illustrated by the Phillips loops in figure 8.4. Although these loops are qualitatively similar to the Phillips loops in the United States, the United Kingdom, and the EC, there is a main difference: the drastically smaller amplitude in the umnemployment dimension, at least until 1991.

Sweden shares this performance to a considerable extent with other EFTA countries. One explanation is probably that small countries with fixed exchange rates become free riders on the anti-inflationary policies of large nations. Small countries may "import" lower inflation from the world market when large countries pursue an anti-inflationary policy. This may be a partial explanation for the only modest increase in unemployment in the small EFTA countries in the 1970s and 1980s: these countries did not have to pursue restrictive policies themselves in order to bring down inflation. Some of them (in particular Norway, Sweden, and Finland), however, have occasionally generated their own inflation bubbles by devaluations, often undertaken in order to boost domestic production and employment in the tradable sector.

Employment-promoting policies in Sweden in the 1970s are illustrated schematically in figure 8.5a, using the basic LD-WS model. As in other countries, unemployment tended to increase in Sweden in the mid-1970s (more specifically over 1976–1978) and again in the early 1980s (over 1980–1983). The conventional explanation among Swedish economists (including me) is that the country ran into an overvalued exchange rate because of the inconsistencies between a slow rate of productivity growth and huge increases in hourly labor costs. In terms of the schematic representation in figure 8.5a, the aggregate Swedish labor market in the mid-1970s wound up in a situation that may be described by point a, with the product wage rate w_1, rather than quasi-equilibrium point c. This, of course, is the conventional wage gap explanation of unemployment.

In order to fight unemployment, the Swedish government succeeded in shifting the aggregate labor demand relation to the right (from LD to LD' in the figure) by huge increases in ordinary and temporary public sector employment. (Ordinary public sector employment increased from about 20 to about 30 percent of total employment.) Selective subsidies to private firms also contributed to this shift. As a consequence, unem-

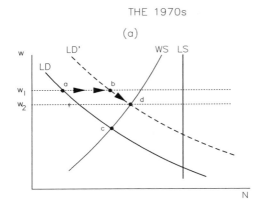

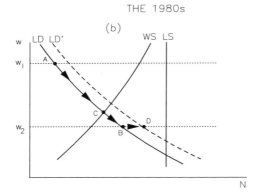

Figure 8.5
Swedish full-employment policy

ployment fell at the prevailing product wage, w_1. This effect may be depicted schematically as a change from point a to point b in figure 8.5.

Moreover, due to three devaluations in 1976 and 1977, the product wage was reduced, and as a result the wage-employment point moved further to the southeast, say to d, along the new labor demand curve. Such a reduction would also be expected to occur without devaluations, but my assertion is that the downward adjustment of the product wage was speeded up by the devaluations. Moreover, by introducing large-scale early retirement schemes for workers, the tendency toward a rise in aggregate labor supply, due particularly to increased labor force participation of married women, was mitigated. As a result, the aggregate labor supply curve was approximately unchanged.

Thus, unemployment in Sweden was kept down in the late 1970s mainly by an expansion of public sector employment and to some extent by devaluations that reduced the product wage. When Sweden again experienced tendencies toward increased unemployment in the early 1980s, the unemployment threat was counteracted by two more huge devaluations (in 1981 and 1982), which combined amounted to about 27 percent (although a temporarily rising dollar mitigated the effective devaluation until about 1985). Schematically, in the context of figure 8.5b, the wage-employment point moved from A to B along a given labor demand curve. Thus, the product wage moved from a point above to a position below the quasi-equilibrium point (at C). There were also some additional increases in public sector employment, which shifted the labor demand relation to the right and moved the economy to a point like D in the figure, at extremely low unemployment rates (1.5 percent).

The overheated labor market in the late 1980s generated, as expected, a new rapid increase in nominal wages and (with a fixed exchange rate) the product wage. However, all major political parties agreed in the early 1990s that the new cost crisis should not be counteracted by either increased public sector employment or new devaluations. The latter position was reinforced when the Social Democratic government announced in November 1990 that Sweden intended to apply for membership in the Common Market, and in May 1991 the same government tied the Swedish krona unilaterally to the ECU (European Currency Unit). The predictable consequence was a combination of increased open unemployment, amounting to about 5 percent in mid-1992, and a strong increase in public works and retraining programs, amounting to about 3.5 percent of the labor force; in mid-1992, no less than 8.5 percent of the labor force was outside ordinary employment.

The Swedish mobility-enhancing labor market policy could not do much under these circumstances. As soon as Sweden started to pursue the same type of anti-inflationary, or "nonaccommodating," policy as most other OECD countries already in the early 1980s, in order to squeeze out inflation, the result was a huge and rapid rise in unemployment.

Thus, I argue that the relatively low unemployment in Sweden in the 1970s and 1980s was linked to three main factors: (1) Sweden could, along with some other small countries, take free rides on the anti-inflationary policies of large countries, hence avoiding very restrictive, unemployment-creating demand management policies, (2) the devaluations in 1966, 1977, 1981, and 1982 helped keep up the employment level in the tradable sector for a considerable period of time by way of reduced product wages, and (3) the large increase in permanent and temporary public sector employment boosted aggregate employment (at given product wage).

Why, then, was the previous policy not sustainable? One reason was that rapid inflation, generated by the recurring devaluations, distorted the allocation of resources, partly because of the nominalistic nature of the tax system. There were also arbitrary, and highly controversial, redistributions of wealth, partly because after-tax interest rates did not adjust fully to inflation. Moreover, between the devaluations, the economy was sometimes exposed to an overvalued currency, resulting in contraction of the tradable sector, and on other occasions to an undervalued exchange rate with exceptionally high profitability in the tradable sector and a reallocation of resources to that sector.

It has also been widely argued in Sweden that the easy profits obtained after the devaluations tended to reduce the pressure on firms to remove various types of slack and that this contributed to the slow rate of productivity growth in the 1980s. In addition, there are long-term costs associated with strong expansion of public sector employment (to the extent that more resources are devoted to the public sector than is consistent with citizens' preferences).

These explanations for the low unemployment level in Sweden in the 1970s and 1980s differ strongly from conventional interpretations, in particular as pursued by foreign observers, who have often singled out three other explanations instead: (1) the (assertedly) centralized system of wage bargaining and the related corporatist structure of wage formation, (2) an activist labor market policy, and (3) the administration of the Swedish unemployment benefit system—issues to be discussed below.

General Policy Implications

In this book, unemployment has been considered in a macro-economic perspective, albeit with a great consideration for the microeconomic foundations. The experiences from various countries certainly illustrate the importance of macroeconomic shocks for changes in the level of unemployment. Obvious illustrations are the gobal unemployment crises in the 1920s, 1930s, 1970s, and 1980s. More specific illustrations are provided by the experiences of exchange rate policies in various countries, such as the attempts to pursue hard currency policies in spite of huge domestic cost increases. Also, the experiences in the Nordic countries, which are often interpreted in terms of microeconomic or structural features in the labor market, are best understood in terms of the macroeconomic policies pursued. For instance, for a considerable time, unemployment was kept down, as compared to other countries, by devaluations and increased public sector demand for labor, but it increased rapidly when these macroeconomic policies could not be sustained.

What, then, are the main policy conclusions of the analyis in this book? If fluctuations in aggregate employment, as suggested by new classical macroeconomics and new real business cycle theories, would be the outcome of optimum adjustments by households and firms to changes in technology and (possibly misconceived) changes in relative prices, such fluctuations should probably not be regarded as a social problem that calls for policy actions. Indeed, as illustrated by Lucas (1987), the welfare loss of the representative citizen in connection with ordinary business cycles in this kind of framework is quite trivial.

An altogether different situation arises if the fluctuations are interpreted in the context of a nonmarket-clearing labor market, because the labor market is then characterized by excess supply and related job rationing. Moreover, some workers (outsiders) carry a much heavier burden than others (insiders); the probability of being employed in the near future is much lower for the former than for the latter. Indeed, it may be argued that the social problem of unemployment is quite closely linked to this asymmetry between insiders and outsiders. If all workers would share equally the loss of jobs and the risk of being unemployed in the near future, unemployment would probably be regarded as a much less severe social problem than is usually the case today.

In terms of a nonmarket-clearing interpretation of the labor market, it is reasonable to regard unemployment as a major macroeconomic distortion, in particular when aggregate unemployment persists for many years and the unemployment spells of individual workers are long. Unemployment may also be regarded as a major microeconomic distortion, as unemployment varies strongly between production sectors and regions, as well as between different population groups and individual citizens. Unemployment is also a psychological and health problem; there is evidence that serious mental and physical effects arise among some unemployed workers.

Against this background it is certainly more important to analyze the consequences of huge macroeconomic shocks, which are often related to unique historical events, and the persistence of the unemployment effects of such shocks, than to study short-term fluctuations in unemployment in connection with ordinary business cycles. Policies that avoid huge increases in aggregate unemployment to begin with or that speed up the adjustment to the initial (or desired) quasi-equilibrium after a huge rise in unemployment, before persistence mechanisms have had much time to operate, may be regarded as investment in low unemployment in the future. This is perhaps the most important lesson from recent empirical experience and contemporary developments of the theory of employment and unemployment, for it is quite likely that the costs of persistently high unemployment are often much larger than the costs of avoiding the emergence of high unemployment in the first place.

From this point of view, the ideal type of policy would be to counteract undesired, unemployment-creating shocks as soon as they arise. Demand shocks would then be dealt with by demand management policies, along traditional Keynesian lines, and supply shocks would be alleviated, for instance, by changes in indirect taxes on production, such as payroll taxes. In the case of both kinds of shocks, various types of labor market policies should certainly also be pursued according to this view.

This way of arguing, however, is largely wishful thinking. First, there are not only market failures but also policy failures. Indeed, it is easy to provide examples of macroeconomic policy interventions in the past that have either been counterproductive or have given rise to severe economic costs and even hardship. In particular, time lags and uncertainties regarding the effects of policy interventions (as emphasized particularly by Milton Friedman), as well as opportunistic policy actions prompted by party politics, are serious obstacles to welfare-improving stabilization policies. The limitations of discretionary stabilization policy have also been highlighted by demonstrations of likely adjustments of individual behavior to (expected) systematic government or central bank policies—the Lucas critique—as well as time-consistency and credibility problems of economic policy.

Short-term variations in temporary public works and retraining programs may avoid some of these problems, because the government itself can simply employ or train workers who would otherwise be unemployed, which means that the positive employment effects seem straightforward in this case. Experiences in the Scandinavian countries also illustrate that fine tuning of public works programs is possible in the sense that such programs (at least in these countries) can be expanded or contracted quite quickly. It is an open question whether such programs can also be administered in an equally flexible way in large countries such as the United States.

These policies, however, are not risk free. Private employment tends to be crowded out by the consequences of such programs for wage formation, and possibly also due to higher interest rates or tax increases in connection with such policies. Another obvious problem with attempted temporary increases in public sector employment is that such policies may, in fact, result in a permanent increase, since political difficulties in cutting public sector employment may generate a ratchet effect. Higher taxes to finance increased public sector employment may result in weak output growth due to the distortionary effects of the taxes. In fact, output growth might then turn out to be so slow that the labor market would become overheated, even with rather modest demand expansion. This is a tempting interpretation of the Swedish experience in the late 1980s, when the labor market became overheated after only a modest expansion of aggregate output.

Under these circumstances, it is reasonable to subscribe to the prevailing skepticism toward fine tuning of monetary and fiscal policy actions, if such policies are interpreted as very ambitious attempts to counteract even modest fluctuations in aggregate

employment and unemployment. These objections to stabilization policy activism, however, are less important when there
are what may be called major macroeconomic level problems—
situations in which the economy is either clearly overheated, as
in the United States in the mid-1960s, Norway in the mid-
1980s, and Sweden in the late 1980s, or in which unemployment is far above the long-run trend, as in several EC countries
in the early and mid-1980s. In such cases, it does not matter
much whether the size and timing of policy actions are far from
perfect from a cyclical point of view. Thus, although it may be
advisable to avoid fine tuning in stabilization policy, there is
a case for "coarse tuning": policies designed to avoid serious
macroeconomic level problems.

The Lucas critique has some clout, however, also with respect
to coarse-tuning policies. For instance, expectations that the
government will try to avoid heavy unemployment certainly
prevent private agents, such as labor unions, from becoming
afraid to push up wages. (An obvious illustration is when labor
unions and employers expect the government to devalue as
soon as a domestic cost crisis results in higher unemployment.)
This highlights the trivial but important truth that objections
can be launched against any economic policy strategy, even
against the strategy of doing nothing, because such policies
may generate persistently high unemployment.

Another important complication for national stabilization policy has been recognized increasingly in connection with the
growth of international capital markets and the removal of
controls on capital movements. Attempts to expand domestic
product demand by way of reduced taxes or higher public
sector spending and related increases in the government budget
deficits seem to create expectations in some countries that the

national currency will be devalued. As a consequence, domestic interest rates tend to go up, sometimes even dramatically.

The easiest way to integrate this idea in the basic model of this book is to include domestic real interest rates (r) in the aggregate product demand function and to assume that this rate is a function of foreign nominal interst rates (i^*), the expected change in the exchange rate $(\hat{e}^e)$, and expected domestic inflation $(\hat{P}^e)$. More specifically, if the domestic nominal interest rate is $i = i^* + \hat{e}^e$, the real interest may be written $r = i^* + \hat{e}^e - \hat{P}^e$. Equation 4.5 may then be rewritten

$$Q_d = K(M/P, eP^*/P, Q, A, r). \tag{4.5$'$}$$

In this analytical framework, apparently expansionary fiscal policies (increases in A) may actually have contractive effects on aggregate demand for domestic ouput, provided exchange rate expectations $(\hat{e}^e)$ react sufficiently strongly to increased budget deficits and domestic product demand is sufficiently sensitive to the higher domestic real interest rates, induced by expectations of devaluations. This reasoning assumes that $\hat{e}^e$ rises more than $\hat{P}^e$.

While in the Keynesian IS-LM model, the induced contractive interest rate effect of fiscal expansion on aggregate demand cannot be stronger than the direct expansionary effects, this can certainly be the case when interest rates are tied to foreign interest rates and expected changes in the exchange rate. Aggregate demand management may therefore be counterproductive in open economies with high capital mobility.

In particular, the history of frequent devaluations in some countries, such as Norway, Sweden, and Finland, has made it difficult for the governments to create confidence in declarations of a fixed exchange rate. Even modest signs that the government may not be able to stick to a restrictive economic policy seem to generate expectations of a new devaluation, with capital outflows and drastic interest rate increases as a result.

Agents in financial markets may also have noticed that the government tends to devalue in response to high unemployment. This means that expectations of a devaluation may arise not only as a result of expansionary economic policy but also in connection with a large increase in unemployment. This catch-22 type of problem seems to have been a basic dilemma of macroeconomic policies in Norway, Sweden, and Finland in the early 1990s.

The policy problem, however, is even more complex. Because increased unemployment, in particular when starting from a very low level, tends to reduce inflation, international competitiveness of the domestic economy may be improved in the future by restrictive policies today, and this may result in lower future unemployment in the tradable sector. A fall in inflation today also reduces political pressure to pursue a restrictive economic policy in the future. Such intertemporal aspects of unemployment complicate life not only for governments but also for economic policy advisers.

These complex interactions between unemployment and inflation, along with the general complications of demand management policies, raise the issue as to whether institutional reforms can improve macroeconomic performance and, hence, reduce the burden on conventional stabilization policy. Let me start with institutional reforms that strengthen the position of outsiders relative to insiders (Lindbeck and Snower 1990a), including both power-reducing policies for insiders and enfranchising policies for outsiders.

Power-Reducing and Enfranchising Policies

Among theoretically conceivable power-reducing policies for insiders, perhaps the most obvious are attempts to reduce the turnover costs of labor. Examples include the softening of job security legislation in order to reduce the costs of hiring and firing labor; such reforms would reduce the gap between the insider and the entrant demand curves and, hence, reduce the market power of insiders. Other examples are laws that punish (by way of fines) strikes during contract periods (wildcat strikes), as well as strikes and blockades against third parties, including firms that use unorganized labor. Revocation of laws that make collective wage contracts binding for nonorganized workers is another example. The government may initiate new laws that prohibit closed shops in the labor market. Another conceivable reform to reduce insiders' market power is to force incumbent workers to finance the unemployment benefit system (for instance, through earmarked taxes on wage incomes).

Such power-reducing policies are particularly important in countries where insiders not only have great power in wage formation, but also use this power without much concern for outsiders. In terms of figure 4.1a, the expected result of such reforms is to generate a downward shift of the wage-setting curve, or at least limit upward shifts.

Power-reducing policies are not Pareto improving. They benefit outsiders at the expense of reducing insiders' real wages or job security, or both. For this reason, current insiders have an incen-

tive to resist such policies, for instance, by engaging more ener-
getically in rent-creating activities.[1]

The social usefulness of power-reducing policies for insiders
also has to be judged on the basis of considerations not encom-
passed by insider-outsider models, or other "economic" models for that matter. For instance, high job security for insiders
through legislation is a social target in itself. Moreover, the
power position of insiders and their unions may have values
outside the realm of wage formation, for instance, in terms of
improving the work environment and protecting employees
against arbitrary treatment. Attempts to restrict insider market
power are also bound to result in political confrontations between the government and insiders, as well as their unions, and
this may certainly be detrimental to peaceful social conditions.

The effectiveness of such power-reducing policies in various
countries is also an open question. For instance, how effective were the attempts by the Thatcher government to reduce
insider and union power in the United Kingdom, and what
were the consequences for wage formation and unemployment?
Clearly, unemployment fell very fast in the United Kingdom
from the mid-1980s. It is impossible to determine, however, the
extent to which this was a result of expansionary demand management policies, tougher labor union legislation and stiffer
rules for obtaining unemployment benefits, or both.

Enfranchising policies are probably less controversial. The importance of such policies is enhanced by the heterogeneity of
jobs and workers, and the failure of relative wages (for reasons
given earlier) to adjust fully to differences in skills and job
characteristics, as well as to geographical mismatches between
demand and supply of labor (although there is hardly any evi-

dence that such mismatches increased during the 1970s and 1980s).

The most obvious examples of enfranchising policies are perhaps those designed to raise the marginal product of outsiders, such as improved vocational training of unemployed workers, possibly in connection with apprenticeship systems, which also tend to keep down the entrance wage for unskilled youth and presumably allow more hiring of young outsiders. Germany and Austria are examples of countries that pursue such policies; these arrangements may be one explanation for the relatively low level of youth unemployment in these countries.

Improvement in nationwide labor market exchange systems and reforms that increase the mobility of labor are potentially important policy actions to help outsiders get jobs, particularly in countries where relative wages are highly distorted relative to skill differentials. For instance, the unemployment of low-skilled labor and workers in declining sectors and geographical regions could probably be reduced if labor unions would accept larger and more flexible wage differentials between skilled and unskilled workers, as well as between different parts of the labor market. A similar effect may be brought about if union power were reduced, the coverage of union contracts were limited, or both. A better-functioning housing market is also an obvious example.

Yet another instance of enfranchising policies for outsiders is reform that stimulates firms and employees to introduce productivity-related wage contracts, possibly in the form of profit-sharing arrangements, so that wages would fall automatically in response to negative profitability shocks. Such arrangements would be expected to limit layoffs of workers without much seniority in business downturns and to reduce the marginal costs of employing outsiders. This means that the insider-outsider theory lends some support to Weitzman's (1987) suggestion to reduce unemployment by profit sharing. Such policies (like the power-reducing policies), however, may make senior insiders themselves worse off and provoke more rent-creating activities from them.

Another conceivable measure to improve the employment prospects of outsiders is to remove barriers to the entry of firms. Such policies would stimulate aggregate employment both directly, by increasing the number of firms in the economy, and indirectly, by reducing the monopoly power of individual firms. Examples of obstacles to the entry of firms are excessive regulations and red tape, as well as tax systems and regulations that discriminate against new and small firms. Attempts to remove imperfections in capital markets provide another example. Thus, from the point of view of the employment level, it may be important to fight restrictions on competition not only in the labor market but also in the market for products and capital. Prohibiting wage contracts from covering new firms (those that did not exist when the contracts were signed) may also facilitate the entry of firms.

A more controversial method for minimizing the discrimination of outsiders is to stimulate work sharing during periods of unemployment. The advantage could be that the number of insiders would be larger than otherwise after a fall in aggregate demand for labor. Wages would then be determined in the interests of a larger group of employees than otherwise. In this sense, work sharing receives a new type of support from the insider-outsider theory. As we know, however, there are also a number of important objections to work sharing (Calmfors 1985).

Other Institutional Reforms

It is often argued that differences in unemployment performance among countries depend, at least partly, on various dissimilarities in the institutional setup of the labor market. Obvious examples are the unemployment benefit system, the labor market exchange system and retraining systems, and the organization of wage bargaining.

Starting with the unemployment benefit system, it may be noted that the replacement ratio is rather high (often over 80 percent) in most West European countries. Moreover, the duration of benefits is usually quite long (often several years) in most EC countries. The situation is quite different in the United States and Japan, where the replacement ratio is much lower and the duration of benefits shorter (see table 2.3, columns 2 and 3). In Norway, Sweden, and Switzerland, the benefit level (replacement ratio) is as high as in the EC countries, but the duration is more limited.

This is not the only difference in unemployment benefit systems among countries. The strictness with which benefits are granted and kept is another potentially important difference. It is difficult to obtain reliable information on the degree of strictness in different countries; however, well-informed observers generally argue that the unemployment benefit system is more strictly administered in Sweden and Norway than in most other countries in Western Europe. In the former two countries, benefits can be cut off if unemployed workers refuse to accept repeated job offers or offers to participate in retraining programs.

If we would like to have an unemployment benefit system that does not raise the quasi-equilibrium unemployment rate too much and does not generate much unemployment persistence, the choice is probably between either a system with small benefits and a short period during which the benefits may be received (such as in the United States) or a system with strictly administered benefits, in the sense that people are denied benefits if they refuse offers of a job or retraining (as in Norway and Sweden).

Improved labor market exchange and retraining systems are other reforms that are often advocated to improve employment performance. Indeed, it is frequently argued that these arrangements have helped keep down the unemployment rate in Finland, Norway, and Sweden. It has, however, turned out to be difficult to arrive at reliable conclusions on this issue in empirical studies (Björklund 1990). The reason might be that such programs have run into decreasing returns due to their extensiveness in these countries. However, countries with very limited programs of this type might have something to gain by initiating them. Also the success of retraining and labor market exchange programs requires the availability of ample job slots (vacancies). Otherwise both a nationwide labor exchange system and an elaborate retraining program would not be expected to be very conducive to fighting unemployment. Thus, labor mobility–enhancing policies, as pursued in the Scandinavian countries, are designed to make low-unemployment economies function more smoothly rather than to reduce unemployment in countries where the unemployment rate is already quite high.

It is important to realize the quantitatively rather limited role of the highly resource-consuming public sector labor market exchange system in intermediating jobs in Sweden. Studies indicate that this system intermediates only 10 percent of all hiring, in spite of the fact that no other labor market exchanges are allowed. It is not obvious that private labor market exchanges, with services paid for by firms and/or workers, would have accounted for less intermediation, if such exchanges had replaced the existing public sector labor market exchange system.

The Swedish experience suggests, however, that there may be gains from some coordination of the labor market exchange system, the system of retraining, and the unemployment benefit system. This type of coordination is perhaps Sweden's main contribution to the international toolbox of economic policy. Moreover, even if the overall quantitative effects of such policies to reduce statistically recorded unemployment have in fact been modest, they have certainly increased the labor force participation of marginal groups of employees, such as individuals with various kinds of handicaps (largely by way of selective employment subsidies to such groups).

How important, then, is the system of wage bargaining for the level of aggregate employment and unemployment? Reference is often made to assertedly employment-enhancing consequences of what is claimed to be centralized wage bargaining in the Nordic countries. However, the bargaining systems there are much less centralized than is usually believed by foreign commentators. To the extent that so-called centralized wage bargaining does occur in these countries, it is usually not in the form of one super-bargaining process between two large organizations, one on each side of the bargaining table. There are generally three or four separate sets of bargaining—usually one set for manual workers in the private sector, another for white-collar workers in the private sector, a third for state employees, and a fourth for local government employees. Moreover, in addition to such quasi-centralized bargaining, there is often subsequent bargaining on the industry level and always on the firm level. Indeed, bargaining on the firm level, the result of which is called wage drift in the Scandinavian countries, usually accounts for about half of the yearly wage increase. In other words, so-called centralized bargaining in the Scandinavian countries should actually be called multilevel bargaining.

Moreover, if the wage bargaining system in the Nordic countries is supposed to be conducive to responsible wage formation, why have these countries had to rely so much on temporary public sector relief work and permanent increases in public sector employment, as well as various subsidies to avoid rising unemployment? And why has it been necessary to rely so much on devaluations to keep down product wages? In other words, why has assertedly centralized bargaining not been able to deliver more modest nominal wage increases? After all, devaluations have traditionally been regarded as a method of reducing the overall real wage level in systems with strong unions that engage in decentralized bargaining, with rivalry between unions that act independently.

To the extent that the quasi-centralized bargaining in the Scandinavian countries in the mid-1970s and the first half of the 1980s helped reduce product wages, this was not brought about by nominal wage moderation. The mechanism was rather that unions did not ask for full immediate compensation for price increases in connection with devaluations. This, then, is a much more modest assertion of the favorable effects of the (quasi-)centralized bargaining system in the Scandinavian countries than the notion that centralized bargaining in these countries has contributed to limiting the rate of nominal wage increase.

Moreover, the degree of centralization in wage bargaining is hardly less in Denmark, with about 10 percent unemployment in the 1980s, than in the other Nordic countries. And the particularly centralized system of wage bargaining in Finland did not prevent a rise in unemployment to about 15 percent in 1992, after the collapse of trade with the former USSR. Thus, it is dubious to refer to centralized wage bargaining in the Scandinavian countries as a successful method to achieve nominal and real wage moderation.

How do these comments on the situation in Scandinavia relate to the theoretical literature on centralized versus decentralized bargaining, where it is often argued that centralized bargaining takes care of various negative externalities of high nominal wage increases? For instance, it has been asserted that centralized unions try to avoid unemployment-creating wage increases because the union members are aware that they have to pay the bulk of the costs of financing the unemployment benefits themselves and also because the probability of members' becoming reemployed goes down when aggregate unemployment increases. Other arguments have been that envy effects between different groups of employees may be mitigated by central bargaining, that centralized unions are anxious to avoid inflationary effects of their own wage increases, and that centralized unions realize that whatever wage increases they push through also raise the prices of intermediate inputs of firms and hence contribute to unemployment also in this manner. (For a survey of these assertions, see Holmlund 1990.)

I am skeptical about these claims. First, as Calmfors and Driffill (1988) pointed out, the market power of unions would be expected to increase through centralized unions, which by itself tends to raise wages in a bargaining framework. Second, the argument about the advantages of centralization largely neglects the heterogeneity of both labor and the production process. More specifically, the argument often misses the consequences for relative wages. Centralization of wage formation means that decisions are made without the decision makers' having access to specific information about the time and place of jobs and workers—information that is available only on the level of individual firms or workers. This may be a reason that centralized bargaining in the Scandinavian countries has resulted in a drastic compression of skill differentials of wages and in the judgment of many observers, including me, has contributed to severe allocation and productivity problems in these countries, particularly in Sweden. Clearly there is a risk that such a system of wage formation results in mismatches in the labor market and, hence, contributes to unemployment.

The argument that centralized bargaining is able to take care of externalities, and hence increase welfare in society, is quite similar to the argument that centralized price fixing by the government, and indeed central planning in general, is able to take care of externalities and is conducive to welfare. The basic weakness of this argument, in both cases, is that important information and incentive deficiencies of centralized decision making are left out of the analysis.

I also suggest that the notion that a country can choose between centralized and decentralized bargaining may be a misspecification of available alternatives. If all bargaining is decentralized to the level of individual firms, bargaining will (by definition) be conducted at just one level. If bargaining is highly centralized, we would expect it to occur at two or three levels: the central level, the firm level, and possibly an intermediate level (of industrial branches). Thus, assuming that wage drift cannot be eliminated, the issue rather seems to be at how many levels bargaining should be conducted.

I hypothesize that total nominal wage increase is likely, ceteris paribus, to be larger if wage formation takes place on two or even three levels than if it occurs on just one level. In this sense, centralized bargaining may very well be counterproductive to ambitions to keep down the rate of nominal wage increase, as well as the level of the real product wage—in spite of often-heard assertions that central bargaining is likely to take care of various negative externalities of nominal and real wage increases.

Moreover, it is not self-evident that centralized bargaining, when imposed on a country where bargaining used to be decentralized, would result in the same wage behavior as in a country that has spontaneously developed centralized wage bargaining. In the latter type of country, both centralized bargaining and responsible wage increases (to the extent that they actually are responsible) may be joint results of social consensus rather than the responsible wage behavior being caused by centralized bargaining.

There is another even more important weakness of centralized bargaining. In such a system, the central union leadership can exert political blackmail over the government by asking for political favors for themselves as a requirement for their willingness to accept wage moderation. Examples are privileges to strike and picket against a third agent, rights to enforce unionization in nonunionized firms, various tax-financed subsidies to unions (such as the tax deductibility of union member fees), or even a tax-financed takeover of the ownership of shares in private firms by the unions (an idea pursued by the Swedish Confederation of Trade Unions in the 1970s and 1980s).

Although centralized wage bargaining perhaps cannot be recommended, it is probably true that general discussions between unions and employers' associations above the level of individual firms, about the reasonable size of aggregate nominal wage changes, may reduce the risks of high real product wages' generating large unemployment. However, as illustrated by Japan and Switzerland, and perhaps to some extent West Germany, such discussions do not require centralized wage bargaining. Indeed, bargaining occurs at the level of individual firms in these countries.

• • •

Some of the possible institutional reforms have been designed primarily to reduce the quasi-equilibrium rate of unemployment, while others have been aimed at speeding up the return to the quasi-equilibrium level after a disturbance. Practically all of the suggested institutional reforms are well known from policy discussions in various countries, including measures to reduce labor turnover costs and other measures to curtail the market power of incumbent workers and their unions, elimination of minimum wages, stimulation of active job search and retraining, stiffening of the rules of unemployment benefit systems, and others. The analysis in this book, with its emphasis on the distinction between insiders and outsiders, has provided some additional understanding of why such institutional reforms may be conducive to reducing unemployment and why other institutional reforms, such as a shift to centralized wage bargaining, probably are not. In particular, the distinction between power-reducing and enfranchising policies follows naturally from the distinctions bewteen insiders and outsiders.

Institutional reforms such as these are best regarded as complements to, rather than as substitutes for, demand management policies—in particular, demand management policies with the objective of avoiding serious level problems rather than fine tuning. Such demand management is important for the level of aggregate employment and unemployment, because there are potentially powerful transmission mechanisms of product demand shocks to the labor market at both fully flexible and sluggish nominal prices.

Appendix A
Derivation of the
Labor Demand
Relation

Let us assume s identical firms, operating under imperfect competition, each producing a homogeneous good through the production function

$$q = f(n, b) \qquad f' > 0; \qquad f'' < 0; \tag{A.1}$$

where q is output, n labor input, and b a shift parameter expressing labor productivity.

Denoting aggregate product demand by Q_d and aggregate production by Q, the aggregate product demand function is assumed to be

$$Q_d = K(\underset{(+)}{M/P}, \underset{(+)}{e \cdot P^*/P}, \underset{(+)}{Q}, \underset{(+)}{A}), \tag{A.2}$$

which is identical to equation 4.5.

Assuming equilibrium in the aggregate product market ($Q_d = Q$), A.2 is assumed to have the inverse

$$P/M = \psi(Q, e \cdot P^*/P, A)$$

or

$$P = M \cdot \psi(Q, e \cdot P^*/P, A). \tag{A.3}$$

It is also useful to specify how the individual firm expects the output of other firms, and hence also aggregate output, to change in response to variations in its own output:

$$\frac{dQ}{dq} = \mu, \tag{A.4}$$

where μ is the conjecture coefficient. A low μ denotes a highly competitive product market; the individual firm then assumes that other firms will not react much to its own actions.

Denoting the nominal wage rate by W and assuming that the individual firm maximizes profits,

$$z = P \cdot q - W \cdot n, \tag{A.5}$$

the first-order marginal condition gives

$$\frac{dz}{dn} = P \cdot f' + q \cdot \frac{dP}{dn} - W$$

$$= M \cdot \psi(\ ) \cdot f' + q \cdot \frac{dP}{dQ} \cdot \frac{dQ}{dq} \cdot \frac{dq}{dn} - W = 0$$

Hence,

$$M \cdot \psi(\ ) \cdot f' \cdot \left[1 - \frac{\mu}{\eta \cdot s} \right] - W = 0 \tag{A.6}$$

where $\eta = -(dQ/dP) \cdot (P/Q)$ denotes the price elasticity of aggregate product demand and $\mu/(\eta \cdot s) = 1/n_f = m$ is the inverse of the price elasticity of product demand for the individual firm. (m is Lerner's measure of the degree of monopoly power.) Also, let the (real) product wage be defined as $w = W/P$.

Recalling that $P = M \cdot \psi(\ )$, it is useful to rewrite equation A.6 as

$$f'(n) \cdot (1 - m) = W/[M \cdot \psi(\ )] = W/P^d = w^d. \qquad \text{(A.6a)}$$

where P^d and w^d now denote the price and (real) product wage "demanded" by the firm.

Let the implicit microeconomic labor demand function in equation A.6a be written in explicit form as

$$n_d = f'^{-1}(w/(1 - m)). \qquad \text{(A.6b)}$$

Multiplying equation A.6b by the number of firms, the aggregate labor demand function may be written

$$N_d = s \cdot f'^{-1}(w/(1 - m)). \qquad \text{(A.6c)}$$

This is simply an explicit formulation of function 4.2.

Appendix B
Price and Wage
Dynamics

This appendix shows that the quasi-equilibirum rate of unemployment (QERU) in chapter 4 is stable under reasonable condition, using traditional assumptions about wage and price dynamics. Let the static macro model in the text, defined by equations 2.2, through 3.1 be combined with the wage and price movement equations,

$$\hat{W} = X(N/\overline{N}) + \alpha\hat{P} \qquad N/\overline{N} \leq 1 \qquad \text{(B.1)}$$
$$\underset{(+)}{}$$
$$\hat{P} = Y(Q_d/Q) + \gamma\hat{W} \qquad \alpha, \gamma > 0, \gamma \cdot \alpha < 1. \qquad \text{(B.2)}$$
$$\underset{(+)}{}$$

By substitution, we obtain

$$\hat{w} = \hat{W} - \hat{P}$$
$$= (1 - \gamma \cdot \alpha)^{-1}[(1 - \gamma) \cdot X(N/\overline{N}) - (1 - \alpha)Y(Q_d/Q)], \qquad \text{(B.3)}$$

which is the assumed real wage dynamics in figure 4.1c.

In QERU, depicted by point b in figure 4.1a, where $\hat{w} = 0$,

$$X(N/\overline{N}) = \frac{1 - \alpha}{1 - \gamma} \cdot Y\left(\frac{K(M/P, e \cdot P^*/P, Q, A)}{Q(N)}\right). \qquad \text{(B.4)}$$

Starting from a situation where $\hat{w} = 0$, and hence $\hat{W} = \hat{P}$, a rise in $N/\bar{N}$, combined with a fall in Q_d/Q below unity ($Q_d/Q = 1$ when the product market is in equilibrium), results in a rise in $\hat{w}$ according to equation A.5, as suggested in chapter 4.

Let equations B.3 and B.4 be written

$$\hat{w} = F(w, P), \tag{B.3a}$$

$$\hat{P} = G(w, P), \tag{B.4a}$$

as N and Q are functions of w by equations 4.2 and 4.4, and Q_d is a function of P by equation 3.1.

For simplicity, rewrite B.3a and B.3b as

$$\dot{w} = w \cdot F(w, P) \equiv f(w, P) \tag{B.3b}$$

$$\dot{P} = P \cdot G(w, P) \equiv g(w, P), \tag{B.4b}$$

where $\dot{w}$ and $\dot{P}$ are time derivatives.

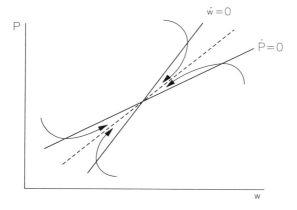

Figure B.1
Stability of price and wage dynamics

The equilibrium point (w_0, N_0, Q_0, P_0) of the static system is then a stable node iff

$$\frac{\partial f}{\partial w} + \frac{\partial g}{\partial P} < 0 \tag{B.5}$$

$$\frac{\partial f}{\partial w} \cdot \frac{\partial g}{\partial P} - \frac{\partial g}{\partial w} \cdot \frac{\partial f}{\partial P} > 0. \tag{B.6}$$

The geometric representation is depicted in figure B.1.

It was argued in chapter 4 that the "own market derivatives" $\partial f/\partial w$, $\partial g/\partial P < 0$. It is also reasonable to assume that each of these own market derivatives, $\partial f/\partial w$ and $\partial g/\partial P$, is (numerically) large relative to the cross-market derivatives $\partial f/\partial P$ and $\partial g/\partial w$. This is the rationale for the assumption in chapter 4 that the LD-WS model is stable.

Appendix C
Alternative
Representation of the
LD-WS Model

Some readers may prefer an alternative graphical repesentation of the LD-WS model to the representation in figures 4.1 and 5.1. Figure C.1 is such an alternative, with the product market expressed in price and output space rather than in real wage and output space. The comparative statics analysis in the diagram is also straightforward.

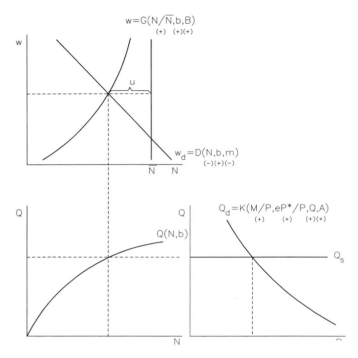

Figure C.1
Alternative representation of the LD-WS model

Appendix D
Wage-Phillips
Curves for the
United States,
the United Kingdom,
and Sweden

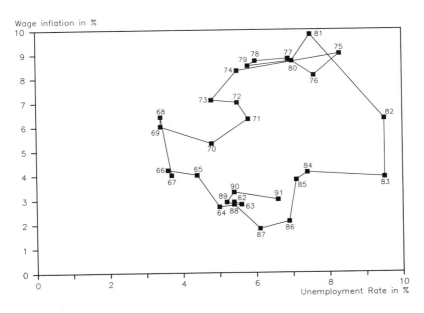

Figure D.1
Wage-Phillips curve for the United States, 1962–1991. Source: OECD, and
Central Statistical Office of Sweden. Note: Wage inflation is defined as the
percentage change of hourly earnings in manufacturing.

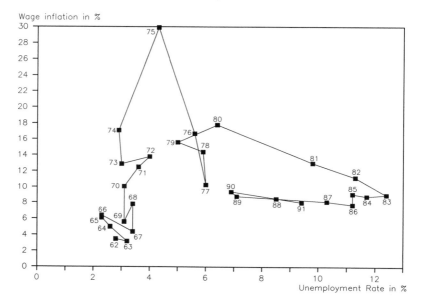

Figure D.2
Wage-Phillips curve for the United Kingdom, 1962–1991. Source: OECD,
and Central Statistical Office of Sweden. Note: Wage inflation is defined as
the percentage change of hourly earnings in manufacturing.

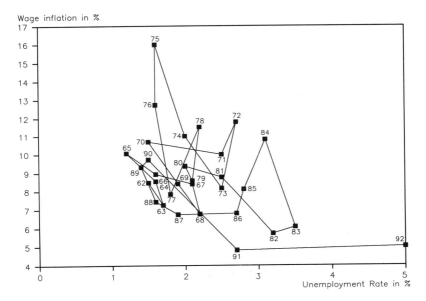

Figure D.3
Wage-Phillips curve for Sweden, 1962–1991. Source: OECD, and Central Statistical Office of Sweden. Note: Wage inflation is defined as the percentage change of hourly earnings in manufacturing.

Notes

Chapter 2

1. This point has been made, and quantified, in Layard, Nickell, and Jackman (1991, pp. 1–2).

2. An exception is the study by Blanchard and Summers (1986) on France, Germany, and the United Kingdom for the period 1968–1984. Alogoskoufis and Manning (1988) also obtained results that are consistent with full hysteresis for some countries.

3. These figures refer to the period 1960–1974. OECD, Labor Force Statistics.

4. In macroeconomic jargon, the United States was characterized by a lower "Okun coefficient" than Western Europe—expressing the percentage change in aggregate output per percentage point change in the unemployment rate. In the 1960s and 1970s, these coefficients were typically estimated at about 2 to 2.5 for the United States and 4 for Europe.

5. In other words, the Okun coefficient was extremely large in Japan.

6. These figures refer to the period 1973–1990; OECD statistics.

7. These studies define the average unemployment spells of all workers in the unemployment pool at a certain point in time.

Chapter 3

1. Price and wage deflation without limits ultimately would create such strong positive real balance effects on domestic spending that these effects would dominate any conceivable negative effects of domestic price deflation on spending through redistributions of income and wealth, defaults of debtors, or negative effects of high real interest rates in connection with expectations about further price reductions. (If the price level would go toward zero, the real value of money balances would go to infinity.) Moreover, although the negative effects of wage and price deflation on domestic spending may very well dominate over the positive real balance effect for many years, it is important to add that wage and price deflation in open economies with fixed exchange rates boosts domestic employment by improving the competitive situation of domestic firms on international markets.

2. See, for instance, Mincer (1976); Brown, Giroy, and Kohen (1982); Linneman (1982); Brown (1988).

3. To do the theory full justice would require a multiperiod (or at least a two-period) model. The discussion here is limited to one period, because several main points of the insider-outsider theory may be brought out in the context of such a simple framework.

4. This assumption is made only to simplify the exposition. It would be enough to assume that insiders succeed in appropriating at least part of the increased "rents" that arise in connection with increased labor turnover costs; the larger the rents are, the higher the insider wage is assumed to be.

5. It may be tempting to argue that the level of employment, through retirement and voluntary quitting, would gradually fall toward the level $\underline{m}$. However, this is not a self-evident inference of the analysis if additional considerations are introduced. Even if insiders would object to outsiders' entering the firm by way of wage underbidding, this does not necessarily mean that insiders would object to the replacement of retiring and quitting workers. Moreover, in the real world, certain types of labor are often complementary to other types of labor, in particular, if the heterogeneity of labor is considered. In this case, it may certainly be in the interest of insiders that retiring and quitting workers are replaced.

Chapter 4

1. In the insider-outsider theory, a specific feature of the wage setting curve of an individual firm is that this curve (like the labor demand relation) is characterized by discontinuities. More specifically, the wage setting curve of an individual firm includes a vertical segment at the initial employment level (cf. Lindbeck and Snower 1990a). This discontinuity, however, tends to be evened out by aggregations over firms.

2. A more compact presentation of the model in this chapter is found in Lindbeck (1992b).

3. A more accurate but more cumbersome name would be the nonmarket-clearing equilibrium rate of unemployment (NERU).

4. Unemployment benefits are not introduced into the product demand function (4.4) because the product demand effects of financing the benefits are assumed to cancel the demand effects of the benefits themselves.

5. Perhaps in a very short-term perspective, the PD curve in figure 4.1b should realistically be modeled as upward sloping, as aggregate product demand in that perspective may be stimulated by higher real wages (at constant Q). This is because the marginal propensity to consume is probably higher for wage income than for profits, in particular, retained earnings. In a somewhat longer time perspective, however, when investment spending would be expected to go down due to falling profits, the relation between Q_D and w may be just the opposite.

6. As there is notional excess supply of labor, it follows from Walras' Law that there is notional excess demand in some other market. Indeed, at prevailing real wages, households would have liked to spend more but are unable to do so because they are income constrained. Thus, there is notional excess demand for products.
A natural extension of the model would be to introduce inventories and to allow "unintended" inventory accumulation as an element of temporary disequilibrium in the product market.

7. The model can be embedded in a larger analytical framework. For instance, by disaggregating domestic demand in an investment function and a consumption function and by assuming that at least the former includes the real interest rate as an argument, a breakdown of output into investment and consumption can be achieved. If we assume that domestic assets are not perfect substitutes for foreign assets, the national saving-investment balance would influence domestic real interest rates.

8. For changes in M to generate a proportional rise in P, it is also required that $e \cdot P^*$ change in proportion to the change in M; then all arguments in the product demand function model would be unchanged.

9. Starting from the quasi-equilibrium point b in figure 4.1a, where $\hat{W} = \hat{P}$, it is assumed not only that $\hat{W}$ falls by a higher unemployment rate (by a lower $N/\overline{N}$) but also that $\hat{P}$ tends to increase when excess demand for products emerges due to the fall in output (when $Q_D - Q > 0$). However, this tendency of $\hat{P}$ to fall is counteracted by the influence of the rise in $\hat{W}$ on $\hat{P}$, and vice versa.

10. For attempts to build such microeconomic foundations, see McCallum (1980) and Mussa (1981).

Chapter 5

1. The real wage rate will necessarily fall as a result of a negative shift of b as $dw/db = (G_N D_b - G_b D_N)/(G_N - D_N) > 0$. Moreover, aggregate employment falls iff $dN/db = (D_b - G_b)/(G_N - D_N) > 0$—that is, iff $D_b > G_b$, requiring that the labor demand function shifts more (vertically) than the wage setting function. (The symbols G_N and the others denote partial derivates.) The effects on the price level are ambiguous:

$$dP/db = \frac{(J_w \cdot (dw/db) + J_b)(K_Q - 1)}{K_1 M/P^2 + K_2 \cdot eP^*/P^2} \gtrless 0.$$

$dP/db < 0$ if $J_b > |J_w \cdot dw/db|$,

that is, if the shift of the product supply curve is large relative to the change in product supply due to the induced change in the product wage.

2. In some countries (such as Japan, Austria, and Switzerland) "remigration" of married women back to the household sector also helped mitigate the unemployment effects of reduced demand for labor. Remigration of workers back to their home countries helped Austria and Switzerland keep down domestic unemployment.

3. $dw/dB = \dfrac{-G_B \cdot D_N}{(1/\bar{N})G_1 - D_N} > 0;$ $dN/dB = \dfrac{-G_B}{(1/\bar{N}) \cdot G_1 - D_N} < 0.$

4. $dP/dB = \dfrac{J_w(K_Q - 1) \cdot dw/dB}{K_1 \cdot M/P^2 + K_2 \cdot eP^*/P^2} > 0,$ assuming $K_Q < 1.$

5. This application of the model raises the issue of whether real money balances in the product demand function should be deflated by P_c rather than by P.

6. See Poterba, Rotemberg, and Summers (1986) for some evidence in support of these short-run predictions.

Chapter 6

1. For a more detailed discussion of this issue, see Lindbeck and Snower (1988b).

2. Monopolistic competition in the labor market, by itself, does not provide microfoundations for unemployment, in the sense of excess supply of labor and related job rationing. To clarify this issue, let us assume that figure 6.1 refers to the labor market rather than the product market. A syndicate of workers that supply labor is confronted with the labor demand curve $d_1 d_1$. If the marginal costs (marginal disutilities) of supplying labor are depicted by the curve MC_1, the syndicate would choose to supply q_1 of labor at the wage rate p_1. Clearly, nothing is gained by saying that such a situation is characterized as unemployment, because the syndicate regards the employment-wage combination (q_1, p_1) as the best one for its members. The fact that individual households would have liked to have chosen a point on the household labor supply curve, if there had instead been perfect competition in the labor market, is irrelevant in this context.

3. Generally the menu cost argument seems to overexploit the envelope properties of profit maximization analysis.

4. It might be argued that this asserted bias can be rationalized by Robert Lucas's "imperfect information" hypothesis in the context of a model with perfect competition, expressing misunderstandings among firms concerning relative price changes. Writing the product supply function of an individual firm $Q = F^*(W/P, P_i/P)$, where P is the output price of the firm and the vector P_i depicts prices of its intermediate inputs, the hypothesis is that the firm observes changes in P faster than in P_i, possibly because it uses thousands of different intermediate products, each bought on different occasions. As a result, the firm may be asserted to believe that an observed rise in P reflects a rise in the relative price of its output. Thus, we would have an application of a Lucas-type "signal extraction problem."

Chapter 7

1. Blanchard and Summers (1986), as well as Gottfries and Horn (1987), formulate their insider-outsider models as special cases of union models, with asymmetric influences on wage formation by incumbent workers and unemployed workers through membership dynamics: workers are assumed to lose their membership status when they lose their jobs. However, in these types of insider-outsider models, the question of where the market power of labor unions comes from is not explained; for instance, there are no labor turnover costs in these models that could explain insider market power.

2. One example is a model by Lindbeck and Snower (1991, pp. 23–24), which suggests that unemployment, under certain conditions, is more persistent in recessions than in booms, in the sense that the labor market may be less responsive to favorable shocks in a recession than to unfavorable shocks in a boom. The condition is that hiring and firing costs, the productivity differential between insiders and outsiders, and the bargaining strength of insiders are all sufficiently large.

Chapter 8

1. Possibilities and difficulties of overcoming this conflict between insiders and outsiders through new contracts are discussed in Lindbeck and Snower (1988) and Lindbeck (1992).

References

Abramovitz, M. 1991. "The Postwar Productivity Spurt and Slowdown. Factors of Potential and Realization." In *Technology and Productivity*, pp. 19–36. OECD: Paris.

Akerlof, G. 1982. "Labor Contracts as Partial Gift Exchange." *Quarterly Journal of Economics* 97:543–569.

Alogoskoufis, G. S. 1989. "The Rise and Fall of European Unemployment." Mimeo. London: Birkbeck College and CEPR.

Alogoskoufis, G. S., and Manning, A. 1988. "On the Persistence of Unemployment." *Economic Policy* 7 (October): 427–469.

Artus, J. R. 1984. "The Disequilibrium Real Wage Hypothesis: An Empirical Evaluation." *International Monetary Fund Staff Papers* 31: 249–302.

Bénassy, J. P. 1976. "The Disequilibrium Approach to Monopolistic Price Setting and General Monopolistic Equilibrium." *Review of Economic Studies* 43:69–81.

Bénassy, J. P. 1982. *The Economics of Market Disequilibrium.* New York: Academic Press.

Bentolila, S., and Bertola, G. 1990. "Firing Costs and Labor Demand: How Bad Is Eurosclerosis?" *Review of Economic Studies* 57(3):381–402.

Björklund, A. 1990. "Evaluations of Swedish Labor Market Policy." Finnish Economic Papers 3(1).

Black, S. 1979. "The Political Assignment Problem and the Design of Stabilization Policies in Open Economies." In A. Lindbeck (ed.), *Inflation and Employment in Open Economies*, pp. 249–267. Amsterdam: North-Holland Publishing Company.

Blanchard, O. J. 1983. "Price Asynchronization and Price Level Inertia." In R. Dornbusch and M. Simonescu (eds.), *Inflation, Debt and Indexation*, pp. 3–24. Cambridge, Mass.: MIT Press.

Blanchard, O. J., and Fisher, S. 1989. *Lectures in Macroeconomics*. Cambridge, Mass.: MIT Press.

Blanchard, O. J., and Kiyotaki, N. 1987. "Monopolistic Competition and the Effects of Aggregate Demand." *American Economic Review* 77(4):647–666.

Blanchard, O. J., and Summers, L. 1986. "Hysteresis and the European Unemployment Problem." *NBER Macroeconomics Annual*. Cambridge, Mass.: NBER.

Blanchard, O. J., and Summers, L. 1987. "Hysteresis in Unemployment." *European Economic Review*, Papers and Proceedings 31:285–295.

Blanchflower, D. G., and Oswald, A. J. 1990. "The Wage Curve." *Scandinavian Journal of Economics* 92(2):215–235.

Brown, C. 1988. "Minimum Wage Laws: Are They Overrated?" *Journal of Economic Perspectives* 2(3):133–145.

Brown, C., Gilroy, C., and Kohen, A. 1982. "The Effect of the Minimum Wage on Employment and Unemployment." *Journal of Economic Literature* 20:487–528.

Bruno, M. and Sachs, J. 1985. *Economics of Worldwide Stagflation*. Oxford: Basil Blackwell.

Calmfors, L. 1985. "Work-Sharing, Employment and Wages." *European Economic Review* 27:293–304.

Calmfors, L. 1989. "Inflation och arbetslöshet—en översikt av efterkrigstidens erfarenheter och teoriutveckling" (Inflation and unemployment—A survey of postwar experience and theoretical development). *Ekonomiska Rådets Årsbok*, pp. 9–30.

Calmfors, L. 1990. Introduction to L. Calmfors (ed.), *Wage Formation and Macroeconomic Theory in the Nordic Countries*. SNS Förlag and Oxford University Press, Oxford.

Calmfors, L., and Driffill, J. 1988. "Centralized Wage Bargaining and Macroeconomic Performance." *Economic Policy* 6:13–61.

Calmfors, L., and Forslund, A. 1990. "Wage Formation in Sweden." In L. Calmfors (ed.), *Wage Formation and Macroeconomic Theory in the Nordic Countries*. SNS Förlag and Oxford University Press, Oxford.

Calmfors, L., and Nymoen, R. 1990. "Real Wage Adjustment and Employment Policies in the Nordic Countries." *Economic Policy* 11: 397–448.

Clower, R. W. 1965. "The Keynesian Counterrevolution: A Theoretical Appraisal." In F. Hahn and F. Brechling (eds.), *The Theory of Interest Rates*. London: Macmillan.

Coe, D., and Gagliardi, F. 1985. "Nominal Wage Determination in Ten OECD Countries." OECD Working Paper No. 19. Paris: OECD.

Corden, M. 1981. "Taxation, Real Wage Rigidity and Employment." *Economic Journal* 91:309–330.

Daniel, W. W. 1990. *The Unemployment Flow*. London: Policy Studies Institute.

Gordon, R. 1990. "What Is New Keynesian Economics?" *Journal of Economic Literature* 28(3):1115–1171.

Gottfries, N., and Horn, H. 1987. "Wage Formation and the Persistence of Unemployment." *Economic Journal* 97 (December): 877–886.

Greenwald, B., and Stiglitz, J. 1988. "Examining Alternative Macroeconomic Theories." *Brookings Papers on Economic Activity* 1:207–260.

Greenwald, B., and Stiglitz, J. 1989. "Toward a Theory of Rigidities." *American Economic Review* 79(2):364–369.

Grubb, D., Jackman, R., and Layard, R. 1982. "Causes of the Current Stagflation." *Review of Economic Studies* 49(5):707–730.

Hart, O. D. 1982. "A Model of Imperfect Competition with Keynesian Features." *Quarterly Journal of Economics* 97:109–138.

Hibbs, D. 1977. "Political Parties and Macroeconomic Policy." *American Political Science Review* 71:1467–1487.

Holmlund, B. 1983. "Payroll Taxes and Wage Inflation—the Swedish Experience." *Scandinavian Journal of Economics* 85(1):1–15.

Holmlund, B. 1990. *Svensk lönebildning—teori, empiri, politik* (Wage formation in Sweden—Theory, empirical aspects, policy). Stockholm: Finansdepartementet (Ministry of Finance).

Kalecki, M. 1938. "The Determinants of the Distribution of National Income." *Econometrica* 6:97–112.

Katz, L. 1986. "Efficiency Wage Theories: A Partial Evaluation." In *NBER Macroeconomic Annual*, pp. 235–276. Cambridge, Mass.: NBER.

Keynes, J. M. 1939. "Relative Movements of Real Wages and Output." *Economic Journal* 49:34–51.

Layard, R., and Nickell, S. 1986. "Unemployment in Britain." *Economica* 53(5):121–169.

Layard, R., and Nickell, S. 1991a. "Unemployment in the OECD Countries." Paper presented at the NBER Conference, in Cambridge, Mass. October 17–18.

Layard, R., Nickell, S., and Jackman, R. 1991b. *Unemployment—Macroeconomic Performance and the Labor Market*. Oxford: Oxford University Press.

Lindbeck, A. 1963. *A Study in Monetary Analysis*. Stockholm: Almquist & Wicksell.

Lindbeck, A. 1967. *Monetary-Fiscal Analysis and General Equilibrium*. Yrjö Jahnson Lectures, Helsinki.

Lindbeck, A. 1980. *Inflation—Global, International and National Aspects*. Eyskens Lectures, Leuwen University Press.

Lindbeck, A. 1989. "Remaining Puzzles and Neglected Issues in Macroeconomics." *Scandinavian Journal of Economics* 91(2):495–516.

Lindbeck, A. 1992a. "Macroeconomic Theory and the Labor Market." Presidential address to the European Economic Association Congress. In *European Economic Review*, Papers and Proceedings, March.

Lindbeck, A. 1992b. "Microfoundations of Unemployment Theory."
Labour, no. 3, 3–23.

Lindbeck, A., and Snower, D. 1984. "Involuntary Unemployment as
an Insider-Outsider Dilemma." Institute for International Economic
Studies, Seminar Paper no. 309. Stockholm.

Lindbeck, A., and Snower, D. 1988a. The Insider-Outsider Theory of
Employment and Unemployment. Cambridge, Mass.: MIT Press.

Lindbeck, A., and Snower, D. 1988b. "Transmission Mechanisms from
the Product to the Labor Market." Institute for International Economic
Studies, Seminar Paper no. 403. Stockholm.

Lindbeck, A., and Snower, D. 1990a. "Demand- and Supply-side Policies and Unemployment: Policy Implications of the Insider-Outsider
Approach." Scandinavian Journal of Economics 92(2): 280–305.

Lindbeck, A., and Snower, D. 1990b. "Segmented Labor Markets and
Unemployment." Institute for International Economic Studies, Seminar Paper No. 483. Stockholm.

Lindbeck, A., and Snower, D. 1991a. "Interactions between the
Efficiency Wage and Insider-Outsider Theories." Economics Letters
37: 193–196.

Lindbeck, A., and Snower, D. 1991b. "Price Inertia and Production
Lags." Institute for International Economic Studies, Seminar Paper
no. 494, Stockholm.

Lindbeck, A., and Snower, D. 1991c. "Patterns of Unemployment:
An Insider-Outsider Analysis." Institute for International Economic
Studies, seminar paper no. 520.

Linneman, P. 1982. "The Economic Impacts of Minimum Wage Laws:
A New Look at an Old Question." Journal of Political Economy 90:
443–486.

Lucas, R. 1987. Models of Business Cycles. Oxford: Basil Blackwell.

McCallum, B. T. 1980. "Rational Expectations and Macroeconomic
Stabilization Policy: An Overview." Journal of Money, Credit and Bank-
ing 12: 716–746.

Malinvaud, E. 1984. Mass Unemployment. Oxford: Basil Blackwell.

Meager, N., and Metcalf, H. 1987. "Recruitment of the Long Term Unemployed." Institute of Manpower Studies, IMS Report No. 138.

Mincer, J. 1976. "Unemployment Effects of Minimum Wages." *Journal of Political Economy* 84:S87–S140.

Mussa, M. 1981. "Sticky Prices and Disequilibrium Adjustment in Rational Models of the Inflationary Process." *American Economic Review* 71:1023–1073.

OECD. *Economic Outlook.* Various issues.

OECD. *Employment Outlook.* Various issues.

Okun, A. M. 1982. *Prices and Quantities: A Macroeconomic Approach.* Washington, D.C.: Brookings Institution.

Oswald, A. J. 1985. "The Economic Theory of Trade Unions: An Introductory Survey." *Scandinavian Journal of Economics* 87(3):160–193.

Pigou, A. C. 1927. *Industrial Fluctuations.* London: Macmillan.

Poterba, J., Rotemberg, J., and Summers, L. 1986. "A Tax-Based Test for Nominal Rigidities." *American Economic Review* 76:659–675.

Rotemberg, J., and Saloner, G. 1986. "A Supergame-Theoretic Model of Business Cycles and Price Wars during Booms." *American Economic Review* 76:390–407.

Shapiro, C., and Stiglitz, J. E. 1984. "Equilibrium Unemployment as a Worker Disciplinary Device." *American Economic Review* 74(3):433–444.

Sneessens, H., and Drèze, J. 1986. "A Discussion of Belgian Unemployment Combining Traditional Concepts and Disequilibrium Econometrics." *Economica* 53:89–119.

Solow, R. 1986. "Unemployment: Getting the Questions Right." *Economica* 53:523–524.

Solow, R. 1990. *The Labor Market as a Social Institution.* Cambridge, Mass.: Basil Blackwell.

Stiglitz, J. 1984. "Price Rigidity and Market Structure." *American Economic Review* 74:350–355.

Tobin, J. 1972. "The Wage-Price Mechanism: Overview of the Conference." In O. Eckstein (ed.), *The Econometrics of Wage Determination.* Washington, D.C.: Federal Reserve System.

Weibull, J. W. 1987. "Persistent Unemployment as Subgame Perfect Equilibrium." Institute for International Economic Studies, Seminar Paper No. 381. Stockholm.

Weitzman, M. 1987. "Steady State Unemployment under Profit Sharing." *Economic Journal* 97 : 86—105.

WIDER. 1989. World Economy Group 1989 Report, *World Imbalances*, Helsinki, Finland.

Winter-Ebner, R. 1991. "Some Microevidence of Unemployment Persistence." *Oxford Bulletin of Economics and Statistics* 53 : 27—43.

Woglom, G. 1982. "Underemployment Equilibrium with Rational Expectations." *Quarterly Journal of Economics* 97 : 89—107.

Wyplosz, C. 1987. "Comment." In R. Layard and L. Calmfors (eds.), *The Fight against Unemployment*, pp. 128—130. Cambridge, Mass.: MIT Press.

Index

DATE DUE

~~JUN 1 9 1994~~			
~~APR 2 9 1996~~			
~~FEB 1 2 1996~~			
	NOV 1 2 1998		
			Printed in USA